ART
DECO
KNITS

ART DECO KNITS

**Stylish
knitting patterns
from the
pottery designs
of
Clarice Cliff**

Melinda Coss

BLANDFORD

First published 1990 by Blandford
(an imprint of Cassell)
Artillery House, Artillery Row, London, SW1P 1RT

Text © Melinda Coss 1990
Introduction and notes on pottery designs © Leonard R. Griffin 1990
Photographs of garments © Liz McAulay 1990
Photographs of pottery © Leonard R. Griffin and Michael Slaney 1990

Produced by the Justin Knowles Publishing Group
9 Colleton Crescent, Exeter EX2 4BY

Distributed in Australia
by Capricorn Link (Australia) Pty Ltd
PO Box 665, Lane Cove, NSW 2066

British Library Cataloguing in Publication Data

Coss, Melinda
   Art deco knits: stylish knitting from the pottery designs of
   Clarice Cliff.
   1. Knitting. Art deco designs
   I. Title
   746.43'2

   ISBN 0-7137-2178-2

Design: Vic Giolitto

Typeset by P&M Typesetting Ltd, Exeter

Printed and bound in Portugal

CONTENTS

Introduction 6
Palermo 9
Blue Daisy 14
Butterfly 18
Nasturtium 22
May Avenue 28
Blossom 33
Gibraltar 38
Autumn 44
Sunburst 50
Latona Red Roses 55
Melon 58
Da Silva Bruhn Man's Sweater 62
V-Necked Cardigan with Whisper Border 66
Crocus 70
Crocus Hat 73
Banded Gloves Worked on 2 Needles 74
Four-in-One Jumper 76
Cubist 85
Rhodanthe 92
Abbreviations 96
Yarn Information 96
Acknowledgements 96
Picture Credits 96

Introduction

Leonard R. Griffin
Chairman: Clarice Cliff Collectors' Club

No one could have predicted the strange twists and turns of Clarice Cliff's life. As a poor teenage apprentice, after a long day's work, rather than go home to relax she preferred to stay behind to model lumps of clay she had purloined from the factory. In her twenties she caught the eye of the boss of the pottery; he, uncharacteristically, paid for her to attend the prestigious Royal College of Art in Kensington. His clever promotion of her colourful pottery meant that by the time she was in her thirties she was a celebrity; during this decade of her life she spent many weeks travelling Britain's major cities, appearing in large stores to face both the public and the cameras of the press. The war that overtook her next decade signalled a complete change of style and aspirations; she gave up her busy career to concentrate on being a wife to the man whose factory she had made famous. When late in her life the revival of interest in "Bizarre" ware gave her a chance to be in the limelight again, she declined to leave the Art Nouveau house she had lived in for 30 years, although she did contribute notes and some pieces of her work to the first exhibition celebrating the "Bizarre" years.

Born in Tunstall in 1899, Clarice Cliff spent nearly the whole of her life in the six towns of Staffordshire collectively called the Potteries. The small terraced house in which she lived during her formative years was shared with two brothers and four sisters. From the beginning, however, Clarice showed herself to be the most individual member of the family. She shared a love of dressmaking with her sisters, a necessity rather than a hobby, but her true interests were her work, and her desire to be a sculptress.

The artistic remoteness of the Potteries towns meant that in the 1920s the region's designers were still using motifs and colours left over from the previous century. The designers were middle-aged men who, though very talented, produced intricate designs in a pseudo-Classical or Japanese style. Few outside the Potteries had ever heard of these designers, and the lack of individuality of their work probably contributed to the general slump that hit the area in the late 1920s. In the depression years things got even worse; 30 per cent of the region's working population was unemployed.

One of the notable exceptions to this high level of laying off was the factory of A.J. Wilkinson. During the 1930s the most efficient method of getting in and out of the Potteries was by canal. The Trent Mersey Canal was used by the factories of A.J. Wilkinson and Newport Pottery; the two companies were sited next to each other in the area near Burslem called Middleport. It was here that Clarice spent nearly all her working life.

The Wilkinson factory had an excellent reputation partly because it made its own glazes and earthenware; it produced a mass of vitrified hotel-ware and tableware. In 1920, to increase its production, it had purchased Newport Pottery. The man behind this was Colley A. Shorter. A tall lean gentleman, still very much a Victorian, he could not have known in 1920 that ten years later, in 1930, both he and his factory would have changed so dramatically. The catalyst for this transformation was one of the many young girl apprentices he employed – Clarice Cliff.

Between 1913 and 1924 Clarice had learned all the methods of pottery decoration – lithography, aerographing, banding, outlining and modelling. She caught Shorter's attention: despite the fact that he was now in his forties he was open-minded enough to realize that she had some exciting if unresolved ideas about how to sell more pottery. At Newport Pottery he gave her the opportunity of doing some modelling of fancies and vases; he even financed her to study briefly at the Royal College of Art. She returned from the latter establishment aware that she was never going to be a major sculptress, but also full of ideas to produce some 'modern' ware.

In 1927 she and Shorter put together a scheme whereby they could make use of defective ware from Newport: a few 14-year-old girls on apprentice wages covered the ware in brashly painted, brightly coloured triangles. This cheap and colourful method of decoration caught the eyes of young pottery buyers. Colley Shorter went to considerable lengths to market the ware and establish Clarice Cliff as its designer. After about a year of his innovative promotional techniques she and Shorter achieved the success they had envisaged.

The company attended major exhibitions and trade shows in London each year and Shorter did his utmost to publicize both "Bizarre" ware and Clarice Cliff. He sent teams of girls into shops to do pottery-

decorating demonstrations, while Clarice appeared with hired film and local personalities. Pictures of these events were widely distributed to the press. In those days there was no such word as 'hype' but that was what Colley Shorter was doing – and brilliantly. On every piece of "Bizarre" ware was an elaborate backstamp: 'Hand painted Bizarre by Clarice Cliff, Newport Pottery, England'.

By 1930 Cliff had her own studio at Newport Pottery. Here she did designs in watercolour before taking them through to a large decorating 'shop' staffed by 60 talented apprentices aged 14–16. Aside from four boys from Burslem School of Art, all these staff were young girls. The chatter, and smell of turps and fat-oil were ever present as the decorators painted in a long dull room overlooking the canal. The apprentices earned six shillings a week for working from 8.30 to 5.30 for five days, plus a half-day Saturday.

In due course interest in the simple original "Bizarre" geometric designs began to wane, so Shorter encouraged Clarice Cliff to produce new original shapes and designs. She created a mass of clean shapes inspired by the ideas of Art Deco. These had wonderful names, such as "Bonjour", "Trieste", "Odilon" and "Yo-Yo", there was even a whimsical "Cock-a-doodle-do" cruet set! Some of her shapes can be traced back to the work of Josef Hoffmann, Desny, and the French silversmiths Tetard Frères. However, her simplest floral designs were the ones that achieved the biggest sales among the 1930s buyers: "Crocus" quickly became her best seller, followed by "Gayday", which featured asters. In the early 1930s up to 20 paintresses spent all their time endlessly painting these designs. "Crocus", in various colourways, continued in production throughout Cliff's career.

The sharp Art Deco designs were soon to be replaced by what was to become Cliff's trademark, her 'cottage in a landscape' style, which predominated between 1930 and 1939. These landscape designs owed much to Edouard Bénédictus, a talented but little known French designer whose work she treasured in two folios of *pochoir* (stencil) prints.

One design, "May Avenue", has been linked with a Modigliani oil painting called *Landscape at Cannes*, and she may also have been inspired by the sketch-books of two of her decorators, Harold Walker and Ellen Browne. However, much of her work in this style was original.

She issued a mass of designs based on floral themes. The names she gave these once again showed her interest in fabrics: "Chintz", "Crêpe-de-Chine", "Damask Rose" and so on. Her "Moderne" tableware range was sold with napkins and table-cloths embroidered in the same design as the pottery, and articles featuring her pottery in women's magazines of the 1930s were often accompanied with instructions on how to produce the design on matching tablecloths or teacosies.

By 1932 the factory's catalogue offered over 400 shapes available in any one of hundreds of designs, most of which were produced in several colourways. Design ranges included "Applique", "Bizarre", "Fantasque", "Delecia", "Latona", and "Inspiration". Each of these offered the customer a different style of glaze or pattern, and included a mass of designs; for instance, there were 12 different "Applique" designs produced between 1930 and 1933. Simply by asking her girls to change the colours, Cliff would issue the same basic design in four or five colourways at a moment's notice. The choice was so vast that buyers could easily acquire a unique piece.

Cliff was now able to maintain her own flat at Hanley, which she promptly painted orange with a black ceiling. She also purchased a car, which she had custom-sprayed in a ruby colour and called Jenny. Much of her time had to be spent away at trade shows, so she had to give up dressmaking, instead purchasing her clothes from the top stores in London; Liberty scarves and cloche hats completed her typical outfit.

Shorter continued to use the full talent of all the factory staff to help promote "Bizarre" ware. Six full-size pottery horses were made of iron frames covered in plates, vases and bowls; these "Bizookas", as they were called, were lent to shops both in Britain and throughout the world. The factory carpenters made attractive cut-outs and stands to find some new way of promoting "Bizarre" each year.

Cliff personally supervised the installation of the shows, filling each stand with vases of freshly cut flowers. Queen Mary, a regular attender of the London trade shows, was heard to comment that she thought "Bizarre" ware 'awful'; on learning of the employment it provided, however, she promptly purchased some pieces of "Crocus". Immediately Shorter produced notepaper for the factory mentioning this royal patronage.

In 1933 Colley Shorter masterminded a project as part of an 'Art in Industry' campaign initiated by the Prince of Wales (later Edward VIII). Well known artists of the day were invited to submit designs suitable for execution on ceramics, and these were produced under Cliff's supervision. The backstamps

therefore featured Cliff's name alongside the likes of Duncan Grant, Vanessa Bell, Dame Laura Knight, Sir Frank Brangwyn, Graham Sutherland and Barbara Hepworth. Despite several shows that toured Britain, the ceramics did not sell as well as "Bizarre"; nevertheless, the exercise served to give further publicity to the Cliff name.

During the 1930s weekly production of "Bizarre" ware was about 1500 dozen. During this 'golden' sales decade some 700,000 dozen pieces of "Bizarre" were produced. Exports went to many countries including Australia, New Zealand, Canada, South Africa, Holland, Belgium, Scandinavia, Eire and the United States. This output was achieved by a staff of over 100, not to mention the 'Bizarre girls', who toiled on the dirty archaic site in appalling conditions. They manned the coal-fired kilns and bottle ovens, where the factory turned raw clay and flint into the finished earthenware and produced its glazes. The resulting pieces went to the "Bizarre" painting shop for decorating, before one final firing in the enamel kiln. They were then packed in barrels with straw and loaded onto canal barges for transport to the dealers.

In 1936 Shorter felt confident enough of his protégée's talent to remove the word "Bizarre" from the backstamps on the pieces, thereafter marketing the ware as 'by Clarice Cliff'. At the same time the daring designs began to be replaced by more conservatively coloured and shaped ware – a reflection of the tastes of the consumer in the second half of the 1930s. The young women who painted the pottery nevertheless continued to be called the 'Bizarre girls', but they were eventually split up by the advent of World War II.

Despite the difference in age between Cliff and Shorter, their desire to maintain their success in the world of pottery eventually bound them together romantically. This love had to be concealed until after the death of Shorter's wife, even then their marriage (in 1940) was kept a secret to avoid scandal. Clarice Cliff the one-time working class girl, now became Clarice Cliff-Shorter, the mistress of Chetwynd House, a stylish Art Nouveau residence outside Stoke.

Their marriage and the onset of World War II combined to bring irrevocable changes to both their own situation and that of their talented team. After the war Cliff was never to resume production of hand-painted pottery on the same scale as before, although she did re-employ some of her original 'Bizarre girls', and a little hand-painting continued through to the 1960s. Cliff was content to become Shorter's assistant at the factory, and his wife and friend at Chetwynd House, where she cared for his large collection of antiques. Too old by now to have a family of her own, she encouraged her sisters to bring their children to Chetwynd. Colley Shorter's two children, both of whom had grown to adulthood before their mother's death, never really accepted Clarice.

With no ambitions left to fulfil Cliff now gave up design, instead appointing a paid designer at the factory. She continued to work as a member of the management team until Shorter's death in 1963 when, heartbroken, she sold the factory to Midwinters and retired. She spent the succeeding years looking after Chetwynd House and tending the gardens. She had few friends, as her marriage had cut her off from her social group; occasionally she met some of her 'Bizarre girls' while out shopping. She seemed to yearn for the days when she had ruled her paintresses with a friendly, albeit firm, hand. Interest from collectors of her wares was firmly rebuffed. Indeed, Cliff was the most surprised of all that her crudely painted earthenware should have become collectable.

In the late 1960s, when Cliff's "Bizarre" wares were rediscovered, they fulfilled every collector's dream. They were easily found and inexpensive, and the combinations of shapes, designs and colours were endless. Inevitably competition for the more unusual pieces meant that soon some pieces were regarded as highly collectable while others were virtually ignored. Although at the time no one realized this, as it was almost impossible to date accurately most of the designs and shapes, this distinction marked Cliff's 'golden years' between 1928–35.

Cliff lived just long enough to hear about an exhibition devoted to her work at Brighton Museum in 1972. She died suddenly in 1973. Her death signalled an even greater interest in her work. Now her designs are attracting collectors throughout the world. Midwinter's Pottery reproduced some of her shapes and designs in 1985, and there has been a television series about Cliff's life. Now some of the designs are available to wear. There is an irony here: had she not excelled in ceramics, Clarice Cliff could easily have become one of the leading fashion designers of the 1930s. She would certainly have been amazed that people not only took an interest in her old designs but actually wanted to wear them!

All the projects include a short description of the Clarice Cliff design on which they are based and most are illustrated with a piece of the pottery. However, some of the pottery is now so sought after that in a few cases it has not been possible to obtain pieces for photography.

Palermo

"Applique" was a range launched in early 1930 featuring European landscapes. Unlike the "Bizarre" pieces colour was used all over the ware. The dark rich blue, milky blue, leaf green and mustard colours seem to have been used almost exclusively on "Applique". Initial designs were "Lucerne" and "Lugano", and Clarice Cliff added "Palermo" to the range later in 1930. "Palermo" features a climbing plant heavy with flowers and, in the background, red-sailed yachts on the Bay of Palermo surrounded by green, lilac and purple hills. The design is shown here on a 13in (32.5cm) wall plaque.

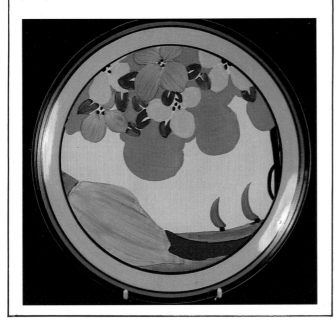

A brilliantly coloured one-size jumper in mohair, worked entirely in stocking stitch using the intarsia method.

BACK
Using 4½mm needles and black, cast on 88 sts and work in k1, p1 rib for 12cm ending on a RS row. P the next row, increasing into every 6th st (102 sts). Change to 6mm needles and begin following chart working straight in st st* to back neck shaping. Work 34 sts, cast off 34 sts. Work to end. Cont on this last set of sts only, dec 1 st at neck edge on the next 2 rows. Cast off remaining 32 sts. Rejoin yarn at neck edge and work second side to match.

FRONT
Work as for back to *, continuing to front neck shaping.
Next row: work 39 sts, cast off centre 24 sts, work to end.
Cont on this last set of sts only, dec 1 st at neck edge on every row until 32 sts remain. Work 1 row straight, cast off loosely.

LEFT SLEEVE
Using 4½mm needles and black, cast on 36 sts and work in k1, p1 rib for 7cm, ending with a RS row. P the next row, increasing into every alt st (54 sts). Change to 6mm needles and cont in st st, working from sleeve chart and inc 1 st at each end of the first and every following 4th row until you have 82 sts. Work 2 rows straight. Cast off loosely.

RIGHT SLEEVE
Work as for left sleeve, but follow chart for right sleeve.

NECKBAND
Join the left shoulder seam. Using 4½mm needles and black and with RS facing, knit up 38 sts from around the back neck, 7 sts down the left front, 24 sts across the centre front and 7 sts up the right front (76 sts). Purl the first row, then work in k1, p1 rib for 6cm. Do not cast off but put the sts on a thread.

MATERIALS
Melinda Coss mohair – black: 125gm; jade: 100gm; orange: 100gm; fuchsia: 75gm; gold: 75gm; red: 75gm; emerald: 50gm; ecru: 25gm.

NEEDLES
One pair of 4½mm and one pair of 6mm needles.

TENSION
Using 6mm needles and measured over st st, 16 sts and 16 rows = 10cm square.

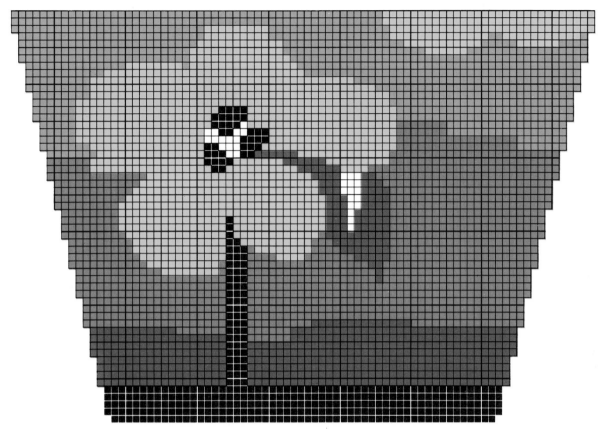

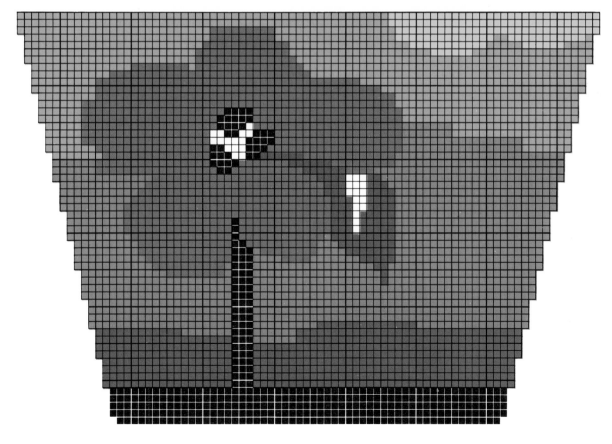

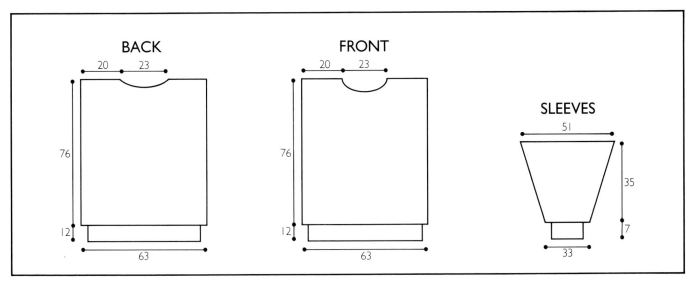

BACK

20   23

76

12

63

FRONT

20   23

76

12

63

SLEEVES

51

35

7

33

MAKING UP

Join the right shoulder seam and neckband edges using a flat seam.

Turn neckband in and sl st held sts to pick-up edge.

Join sleeves to jumper, join sleeve and side seams.

Follow the chart opposite to complete both the back and front of the jumper. The charts for the sleeves are on page 11, follow the top chart to complete the right sleeve and the bottom chart for the left sleeve.

Blue Daisy

"Blue Daisy" was a very untypical Clarice Cliff design. It was painted freehand and probably appeared about the same time as the "Tennis" design in 1931. Clarice Cliff was often under pressure to produce new designs to be sold solely to one chain of stores, and simple ones such as this were perhaps produced for this reason.

A long-sleeved cotton jumper worked in double-knitting cotton using the intarsia method.

FRONT

Using 3¼mm needles and white, cast on 116 sts. Work in k2, p2 rib for 6 rows. Change to 3¾mm needles and, commencing with a knit row, work in st st from chart until the 128th row has been completed. Cast off 5 sts at beg of next 2 rows. Cont following the graph to **neck shaping**.
Next row: k39, slip remaining sts onto a spare needle. Working on this first set of sts only, dec 1 st at neck edge on next 16 rows. Cast off remaining 23 sts. Rejoin yarn at neck edge and cast off centre 28 sts, work to end of row. Complete neck shaping to match first side, cast off remaining 23 sts.

BACK

Work as for front but reverse the image – i.e., read chart from right to left in purl and from left to right in knit.

SLEEVES (both alike)

Using 3¼mm needles and white, cast on 56 sts. Work in k2, p2 rib for 6 rows, increasing 1 st at each end of the last row (58 sts).
Change to 3¾mm needles and, starting with a knit row, work in pattern as follows.
Row 1: k22 blue, k3 black, k3 mauve, k3 blue, k2 white, k25 blue.
Row 2: p25 blue, p2 white, p3 blue, p3 mauve, p3 black, p22 blue.

Rep these 2 rows once more.
Row 5: k22 white, k3 black, k3 mauve, k3 blue, k27 white.
Row 6: inc 1, p27 white, p3 blue, p3 mauve, p3 black, p22 white, inc 1.
These 6 rows form the pattern and should be worked throughout. At the same time, after increasing at each end of the 6th row, inc 1 st at each end of every 4th row until you have 108 sts. Cont in pattern without further shaping until sleeve measures 47cm (completing a stripe). Cast off loosely.

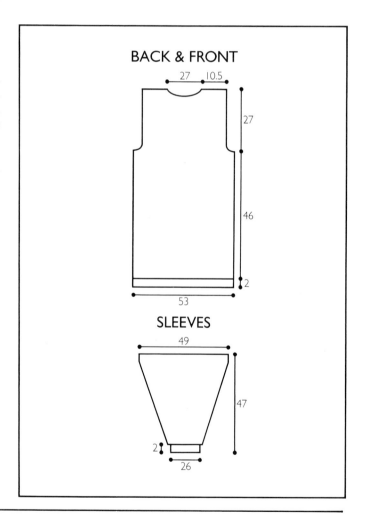

MATERIALS
Melinda Coss DK cotton – royal blue: 550gm; white: 450gm; mauve: 100gm; black: 100gm; coral: 50gm.

NEEDLES
One pair of 3¼mm and one pair of 3¾mm needles.

TENSION
Using 3¾mm needles and measured over st st, 22 sts and 28 rows = 10cm square.

COLLAR

Using 3¼mm needles and white, cast on 20 sts. Work in k2, p2 rib for approx 82cm (or until band fits evenly around the neckline). Cast off neatly.

MAKING UP

Join shoulder seams using a narrow backstitch. Join sleeves to shoulders taking care to keep vertical stripes centred at the shoulder seam. Join sleeve and side seams. Pin the two corner edges of the collar to the centre front of the jumper. Sew collar to neck edge along top edge only so that collar has 2 points at centre front.

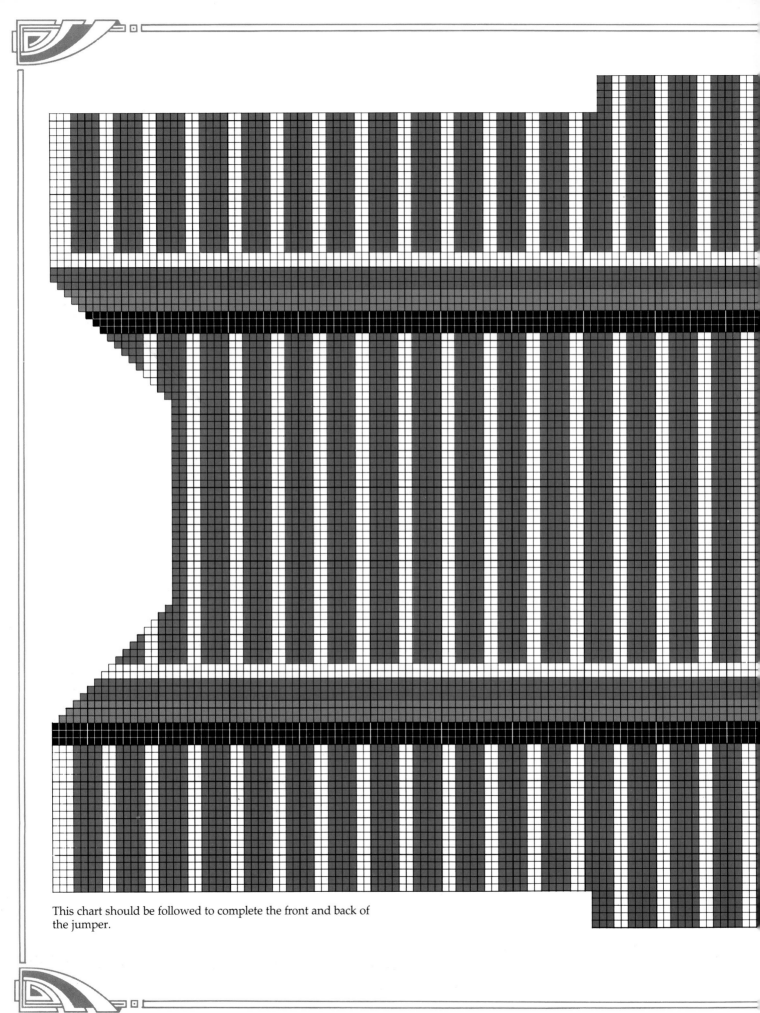

This chart should be followed to complete the front and back of the jumper.

Butterfly

This design was copied by Clarice Cliff from a folio of *pochoir* (stencil) prints by a little-known French designer called Edouard Bénédictus. The freehand butterflies and stripes were identical to the Bénédictus original, and this design ironically appeared in 1930, the year Bénédictus died.

The "Butterfly" motif has been used to decorate this silky evening jacket in 6-ply mercerized cotton.

LEFT FRONT

Using 3¼mm needles and M, cast on 70 sts and work in moss st for 2cm ending with WS facing. P 1 row. Now with RS facing, set stripes pattern as follows:
Next row (side edge): k19(D), k21(C), k5(B), k25(A).
Next row: p25(A), p5(B), p21(C), p19(D).
Keeping stripes as set, work 56 rows from left front bottom chart, then cont in stripes until work measures 47cm from cast-on edge, ending with RS facing. **Shape neck:** keeping stripes correct, begin shaping 'V'-neck by dec 1 st at front edge on next and every following 5th row 6 times. Work 3 rows in stripe sequence ending at side edge. Cast on 104 sts at beg of next row for sleeve. Next row (cuff edge): k25(A), k5(B), k21(C), k19(D), k9(E), k25(A), k19(D), k21(C), k5(B), k18(A)**. Now cont in stripe sequence as set for a further 31 rows, dec 1 st at front edge as before on next and every following 5th row (161 sts). Now set top butterfly as follows:
Next row: keeping both stripe sequence and front decs correct (cuff edge), k25(A), k5(B), k21(C), k19(D), k9(E), k4(A). Chart 60 sts, k1(C), k5(B), k12(A). Cont from chart. When 152 sts remain, keep

front edge straight until chart is completed. Cast off all sts in correct colours.

RIGHT FRONT

Work as for left front, working in colour stripes only, setting sts as follows after moss st welt.
Next row (front edge): k25(A), k5(B), k21(C), k19(D). With sts thus set, work in stripes only (no butterfly on this front until placed further into pattern on sleeve) until ** is reached. Now set stripes as follows: next row (WS): p25(A), p5(B), p21(C), p19(D), p9(E), p25(A), p19(D), p21(C), p5(B), p18(A). Now, keeping front dec correct, work left front bottom chart setting sts as follows.
Next row (front edge): k2 tog in A, k16(A), k5(B), k21(C), k19(D), k25(A), k9(E). Chart 70 sts (starting 19(D)). Now with sts thus set and keeping both front decs and stripes correct, work 56 rows from chart, then work 24 rows in stripes only. Cast off all sts in correct colours.

BACK

Using 3¼mm needles and M, cast on 150 sts and work in moss st as on front. Now set stripes as follows:
Next row (RS): k19(D), k21(C), k5(B), k25(A), k10(E), k25(A), k5(B), k21(C), k19(D). Work 3 more rows in stripe pattern, now set butterfly using left front top chart, setting sts as follows and keeping in stripe sequence. Next row (RS): k19(D), k21(C), k5(B), k25(A), k10(E), k10(A), 60 sts from chart (remembering that the background colours differ from those on chart). With sts thus set, work 48 rows from chart, then cont in stripes as set until work measures same as front to sleeve cast-on, ending with RS facing. Cast on 104 sts at beg of next row for sleeve. Next row: k25(A), k5(B), k21(C), k19(D), k9(E),

---

MATERIALS
Melinda Coss 6-ply mercerized cotton.
Black (M): 200gm; beige (A): 300gm; cream (B): 50gm; coffee (C): 200gm; gold (D): 200gm; yellow (E): 50gm; green, white, red and blue for the motifs: less than 50gm of each.
4 × 3cm square buttons.

NEEDLES
One pair of 2¾mm (35cm long) and one pair of 3¼mm needles.

TENSION
Using 3¼mm needles and measured over st st, 26 sts and 32 rows = 10cm square.
Front edges, collar and cuffs worked on 2¾mm needles.

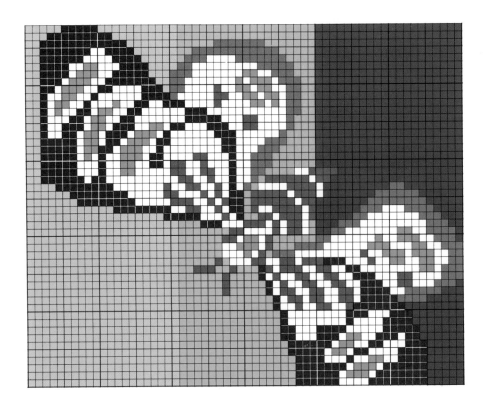

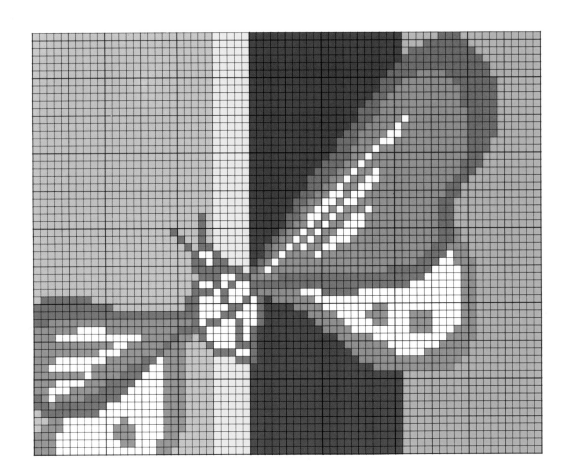

k25(A), k19(D), k21(C), k5(B), k25(A), k10(E), k25(A), k5(B), k21(C), k19(D). Cast on 104 sts for second sleeve. Next row (WS): p25(A), p5(B), p21(C), p19(D), p9(E), p25(A), p19(D), p21(C), p5(B), p25(A), p10(E), p25(A), p5(B), p21(C), p19(D), p25(A), p9(E), p19(D), p21(C), p5(B), p25(A). Now cont with stripes as set until work measures same as front to shoulder. Cast off all sts using correct colours.

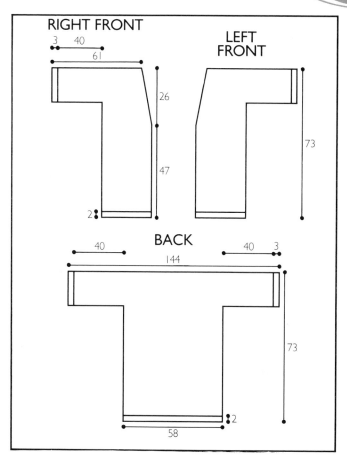

FRONT EDGE (button side)

Mark a point 10cm from cast-off sts. With RS facing and using 2¾mm needles and M, pick up and knit approx 220 sts along front edge from marked point to cast-on edge. Work in moss st for 4cm ending at cast-on edge. Next row: cast off 140 sts, moss st to end, work on remaining sts for revere collar.
Work 1 row in moss st, then cast off 2 sts at beg of next and every following alt row until all sts are worked off needle.

FRONT EDGE (buttonhole side)

Pick up as for buttonside starting at cast-on edge and finishing at marked point. Work in moss st for 2cm finishing at cast-on edge. Buttonhole row: moss 4 sts, (cast off 6 sts, moss 40 sts) 3 times, cast off 6 sts, moss st to end. Cont in moss st, casting on 6 sts over those cast off on previous row, until band measures 4cm ending at cast-on edge. Work as for buttonside for revere.

COLLAR

Join sleeve top and shoulder seams with matching colours. Using 2¾mm needles and M and with RS facing, pick up and knit approx 108 sts evenly between marked points. Inc 6 sts across 44 back neck sts on first row (to allow for ease at back of neck), work in moss st for 7cm. Cast off.

CUFFS

Using 2¾mm needles and M, pick up 100 sts across sleeve edge and work in moss st for 3cm. Cast off. Repeat for second cuff.

MAKING UP

Fold back revere and catch to back collar. Join side and sleeve seams in correct colours. Sew on buttons to correspond with buttonholes.

Incorporate the butterfly motifs opposite into the pattern as described on page 18. Follow the bottom chart for the butterfly on the left front and right sleeve, and the top chart for the butterfly on the left shoulder and on the back of the jacket.

Nasturtium

"Inspiration" was the name of a glaze technique, the designs used with it were standard "Bizarre" landscapes, Persian inspired designs or floral patterns such as the "Inspiration" version of "Nasturtium". "Inspiration" was produced by an entirely different technique to "Bizarre" ware; the surface colours were liquid glazes containing copper, cobalt and iron, which were both difficult to apply and fire. Colley Shorter was particularly proud of this ware and was interviewed about it in 1929, '"Inspiration" has unveiled the secret which was lost for centuries of reproducing in a superb matt glaze, the gorgeous colour peculiar to Ancient Egyptian Pottery known as Scarab Blue.'

An abstract, floral mohair coat, worked using the intarsia method.

BACK

Using 4½mm needles and turquoise, cast on 92 sts and work in k1, p1 rib for 6½cm, inc 10 sts evenly across last row of rib (102 sts).
Change to 5½mm needles and commence following the chart working in st st throughout for 106 rows.
Shape armholes: cast off 9 sts at beg of next 2 rows. Cont following chart to shoulder shaping. Cast off 8 sts at beg of next 6 rows. Cast off remaining 36 sts.

LEFT FRONT

Using 4½mm needles and turquoise, cast on 46 sts and work in k1, p1 rib for 6½cm, inc 5 sts evenly across last row of rib (51 sts)*.
Change to 5½mm needles and commence following chart, working in st st throughout, for 106 rows.
Shape armhole: cast off 9 sts at beg of next row. Work in st st for 4 rows. **Shape neck:** dec 1 st at beg of next row and the 12 following alt rows (29 sts).

Cont following chart to shoulder shaping. Next row (RS): cast off 8 sts at beg of this row and the next 2 alt rows. Work 1 row. Cast off remaining 5 sts.

RIGHT FRONT

Work as for left front to *. Change to 5mm needles and follow chart for right front.

MATERIALS
Melinda Coss mohair –
turquoise: 400gm; mid-blue: 125gm; royal blue: 100gm; navy: 50gm; mauve: 50gm; ecru: 50gm; ginger: 50gm.
6 × 3cm square buttons.

NEEDLES
One pair of 4½mm and one pair of 5½mm needles.

TENSION
Using 5½mm needles and measured over st st, 16 sts and 20 rows = 10cm square.
Ribs for back, left front and right front worked on 4½mm needles.

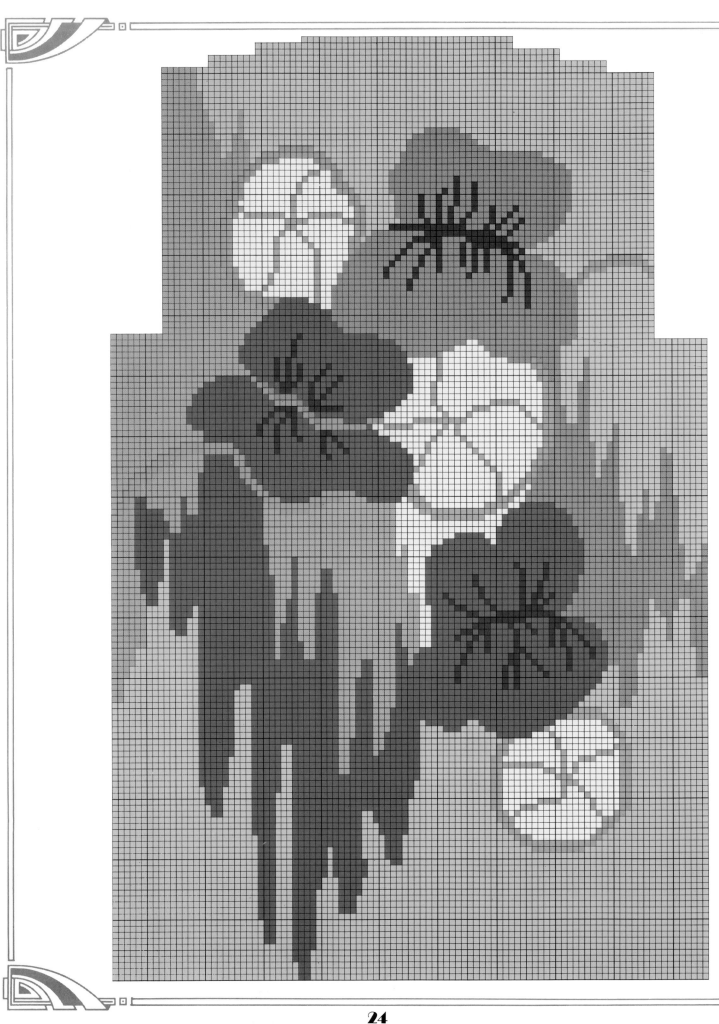

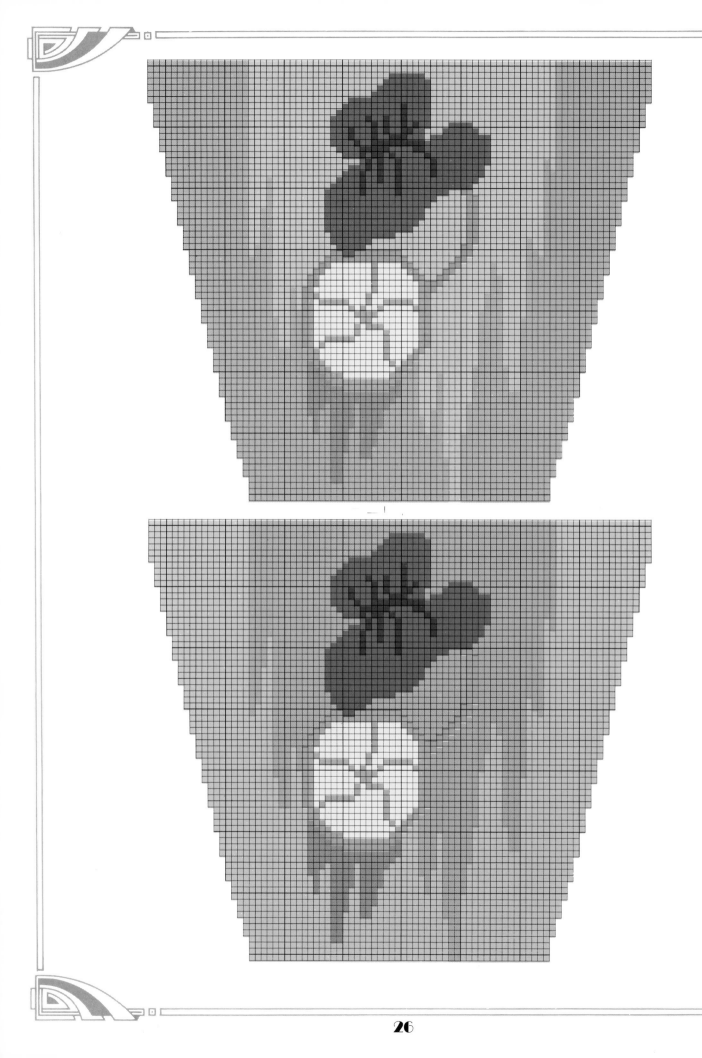

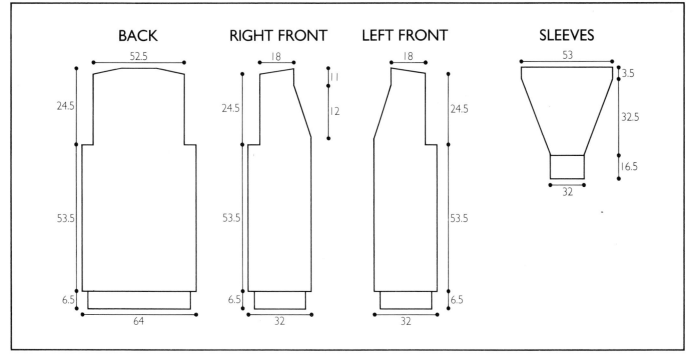

BACK	RIGHT FRONT	LEFT FRONT	SLEEVES

BACK 52.5 / 24.5 / 53.5 / 6.5 / 64

RIGHT FRONT 18 / 11 / 12 / 24.5 / 53.5 / 6.5 / 32

LEFT FRONT 18 / 24.5 / 53.5 / 6.5 / 32

SLEEVES 53 / 3.5 / 32.5 / 16.5 / 32

SLEEVES

Using 5½mm needles and turquoise, cast on 51 sts.
Row 1: k1 (p1, k1) to end.
Row 2: p1 (k1, p1) to end. Rep these 2 rows for 16½cm ending with a 2nd row. Cont following chart using appropriate colours as indicated and increasing 1 st at each end of the 4th row and every following 3rd row until you have 59 sts. Then inc 1 st at each end of every following 4th row until you have 85 sts. Work 7 rows straight, thus completing the chart. Cast off loosely.

BUTTONBAND AND LEFT COLLAR

Using 5½mm needles and turquoise, cast on 18 sts and work in k1, p1 rib until band fits up front edge to beg of front shaping when slightly stretched. Next row (RS): rib 2, inc 2, rib to end. Next 3 rows: rib to end. Rep last 4 rows 12 times more. Next row: rib 2, inc 2, rib to end (46 sts). Work straight until band fits up front edge to centre back neck when slightly stretched. Cast off in rib. Using pins, mark 6 button positions, the first one 3cm from cast-on edge, the last one 2cm from beg of collar shaping and the remainder evenly spaced between.

BUTTONHOLE BAND AND RIGHT COLLAR

Work as for buttonband reversing the shapings by reading RS row for WS row and working buttonholes to correspond with pins as follows. Buttonhole row (RS): rib 7, cast off 4, rib to end. On return row cast on 4 sts over those previously cast off.

MAKING UP

Join shoulder seams, set in sleeves, then join side and sleeve seams. Sew buttonband and left collar, and buttonhole band and right collar, into position and join cast-off edges at centre back neck with an invisible seam. Sew on buttons.

Follow the chart on page 24 to complete the back and the charts on page 25 to complete the left and right fronts. The charts for the sleeves are given opposite, follow the top chart for the left sleeve and the bottom chart for the right sleeve.

May Avenue

There are two May Avenue's in Stoke-on-Trent, one is just a few roads from Clarice Cliff's home town of Tunstall, the other is a couple of miles away. They were undoubtedly the inspiration for the name of this design, but the scene was not inspired by them. Comparison of this design with an oil painting by Modigliani, *'Landscape at Cannes'*, shows too many similar features to be accounted for by coincidence. The spade-shaped trees, cloud-shaped bushes, and red-roofed houses appear in both. Cliff adapted the design slightly by adding a large green and blue tree, behind which the avenue disappears. The "Stamford" shape trio is the only known example of this shape and design combined and dates from 1932 or 1933.

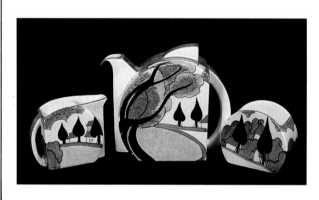

This crew-necked jumper in double-knitting wool has the "Bizarre" trademark stamped on the back.

FRONT

Using 3¼mm needles and black, cast on 120 sts. Work 4 rows in k1, p1 rib. Change to ecru, rib 4 rows. Change to blue, rib until work measures 10cm, inc 18 sts evenly across last row of rib (138 sts). Change to 3¾mm needles* and start following the chart for front, working in st st until you reach the neck shaping. Next row (RS): k56, place these sts on a spare needle, slip centre 26 sts onto a stitch holder, rejoin yarn, k56. Working on this last set of sts only, dec 1 st at neck edge on the next 11 alt rows. Work 7 rows without shaping, slip remaining 45 sts onto a spare needle. Repeat shaping for other side of neck.

BACK

Work as for front to *. Using black only, work in st st for 48 rows. Next row (RS): position back chart as follows: k25 black, k first row (88 sts) of back chart, k25 black. Cont in st st as set until the chart is complete, then work in black only until back measures same as front to shoulder. Hold sts on a spare needle.

SLEEVES (both alike)

Using 3¼mm needles and black, cast on 56 sts. Work 4 rows in k1, p1 rib. Change to ecru, rib 4 rows. Change to blue, rib until work measures 6cm, inc 4 sts evenly across last row of rib (60 sts). Change to 3¾mm needles and black and cont in st st, increasing 1 st at each end of every 4th row until you have 124 sts. Cont straight until sleeve measures 68cm (including rib). Cast off loosely.

MATERIALS
Melinda Coss DK wool –
black: 450gm; ecru: 150gm;
blue: 100gm; yellow, lime
green, apple green, jade, red:
50gm of each.

NEEDLES
One pair of 3¼mm and one
pair of 3¾mm needles. One
stitch holder.

TENSION
Using 3¾mm needles and
measured over st st, 24 sts and
30 rows = 10cm square.

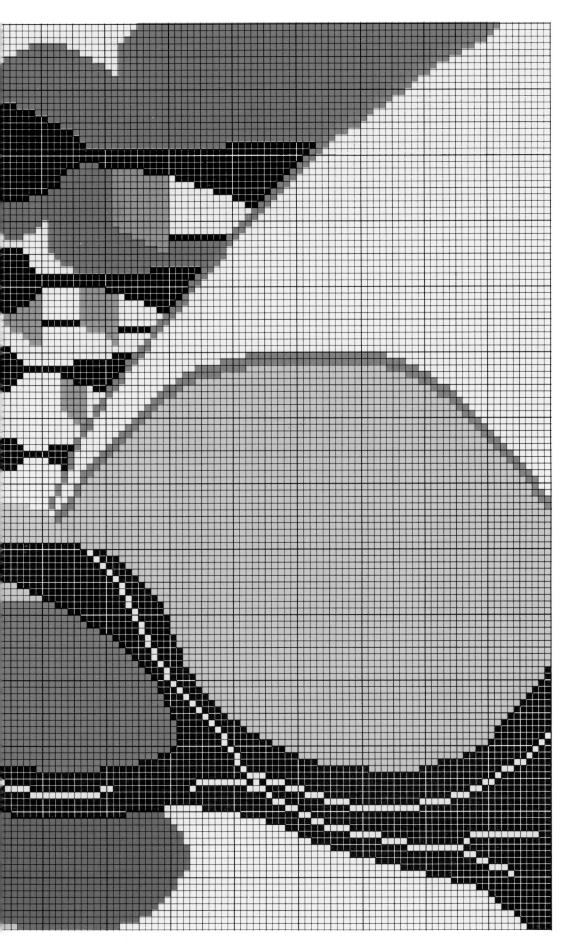

Follow this chart to complete the front of the jumper. The chart on page 32 should be incorporated into the back of the jumper.

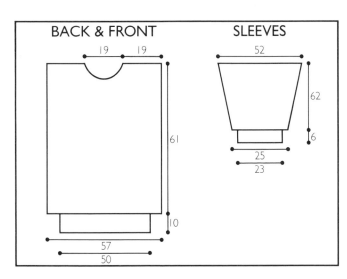

BACK & FRONT

19 19

61

10

57
50

SLEEVES

52

62

6

25
23

NECKBAND

Knit one shoulder seam together. Using 3¼mm needles and black, pick up and k the 48 sts held for centre back, 30 sts down one side of front, 26 sts held for centre front and 30 sts up other side of front (134 sts). Working in k1, p1 rib, work 2 rows in black, 2 rows ecru, 3 rows blue, k 1 row blue, rib 3 rows blue, 2 rows ecru, 2 rows black. Cast off loosely.

MAKING UP

Knit second shoulder seam together. Turn neckband inwards and slip stitch cast-off edge to pick-up edge. Using a flat seam, join sleeves to jumper, then join sleeve and body seams.

Blossom

"Blossom" was used as part of both the "Latona" range, where it was painted onto the milky coloured glaze without the trellis pattern and as part of the "Applique" range where it appears with the trellis. Both examples are rare and the design was produced probably only for samples.

This jumper is worked in mercerized cotton which produces a clear shiny effect that gives the colours a strong definition. It is worked using the intarsia method.

FRONT

Using 3mm needles and gold, cast on 110 sts. Work in k2, p2 rib for 7cm.

Change to 3¾mm needles and follow the chart in st st, starting with a k row and making small bobbles where indicated on chart. When the make bobble position on the row has been reached, make 4 stitches out of the next one by knitting into its front, then its back, front and back again before slipping it off the LH needle. Turn the work and knit these 4 stitches only. Turn the work, purl 4. Using the point of the left-hand needle, lift the bobble stitches, in order, over the first one on the right-hand needle, i.e., 2nd, 3rd and 4th, so that one stitch remains. If worked on a right side row, the bobble will hang on the right side, if worked on a wrong side row, push it through on to the right side. After completing the bobble, the work may continue as normal, the single stitch having been restored to its original position on the row. Work until 61 rows are complete. **Shape armholes:** cast off 2 sts at beg of next 2 rows. Cont straight until 138 rows of the chart have been worked. **Shape neck:** next row (RS): k42, leave remaining sts on a spare needle and, working on this first set of sts only, cast off 8 sts at beg of next row, 4

sts at beg of next 2 alt rows and 2 sts at beg of the following 2 alt rows. Work 2 rows, cast off remaining 22 sts.

Slip centre 22 sts onto a stitch holder, rejoin yarn to remaining sts, k to end. P1 row. Cast off 8 sts at beg of next row, then cast off 4 sts at beg of the next 2 alt rows, and 2 sts on the following 2 alt rows. Work 1 row. Cast off remaining 22 sts.

BACK

Work as for front until back neck shaping. **Shape**

MATERIALS
Melinda Coss DK mercerized cotton – gold: 500gm; ecru: 150gm; black: 100gm; red: 100gm; grey: 50gm; yellow: 50gm; lilac: 50gm; white: 50gm.

NEEDLES
One pair of 3mm and one pair of 3¾mm needles. One 3mm (short) circular needle. One stitch holder.

TENSION
Using 3¾mm needles and measured over st st, 20 sts and 28 rows = 10cm square.

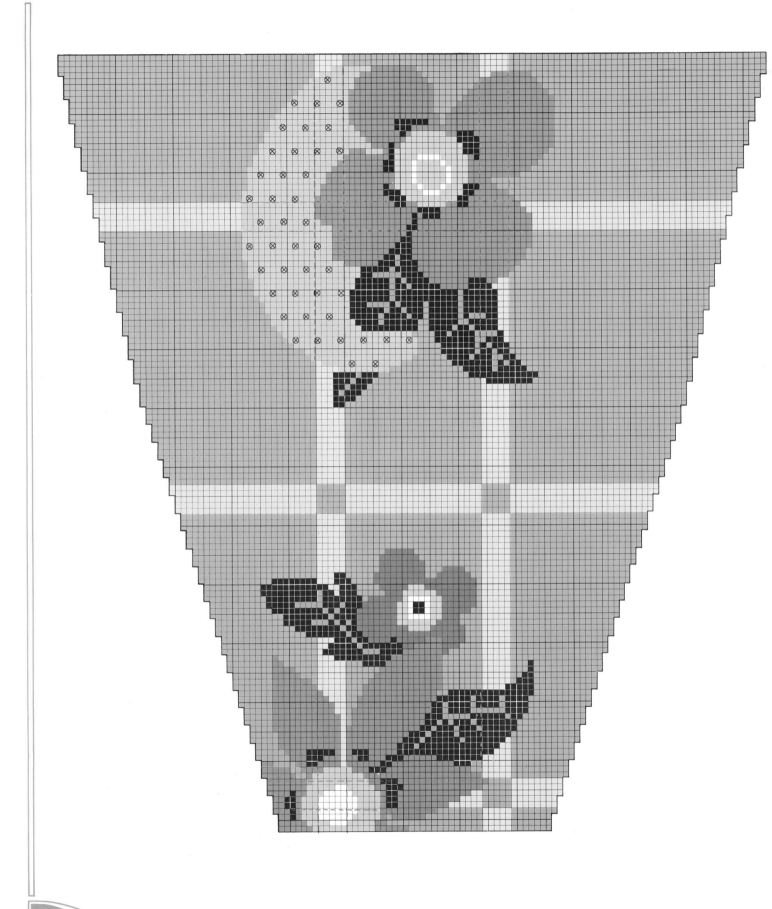

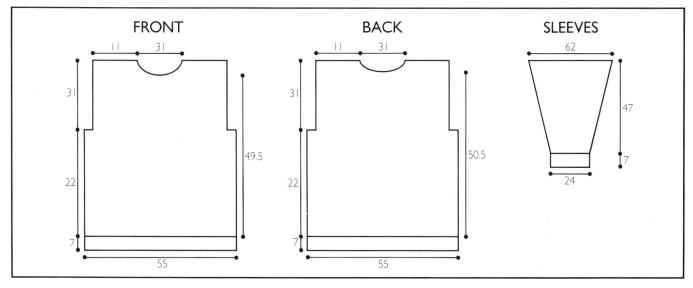

FRONT   BACK   SLEEVES

neck: next row (RS): k30, turn, cast off 4 sts, p to end, k 1 row, turn, cast off 2 sts at beg of next row and the following alt row. Work 2 rows. Cast off remaining 22 sts. Slip centre 46 sts onto a spare needle, k to end. P 1 row, cast off 4 sts at beg of next row, p 1 row, cast off 2 sts at beg of next row and following alt row, p 1 row, cast off remaining sts.

LEFT SLEEVE

Using 3mm needles and gold, cast on 48 sts and work in k2, p2 rib for 7cm.
Change to 3¾mm needles* and follow chart in st st, working the bottom set of floral motifs only but continuing the trellis pattern throughout, as indicated by the dotted lines. *At the same time*, inc 1 st at each end of every 3rd row 24 times (96 sts), then inc every 4th row 14 times (124 sts). Work until chart is complete. Cast off loosely.

RIGHT SLEEVE

Work as for left sleeve to *. Follow chart in st st, working the trellis as indicated by the dotted line but omitting the first set of floral motifs. *At the same time* inc 1 st at each end of every third row 24 times (96 sts), then every 4th row 14 times (124 sts). Work until chart is complete. Cast off loosely. Join shoulder seams.

NECKBAND

Using a 3mm circular needle and gold, and starting at left shoulder point, pick up 108 sts around neck edge, including sts on spare needles. Starting at shoulder point, k2, p2 in circular rib for 2cm. Cast off loosely ribwise.

MAKING UP

Join sleeves to body, join side and sleeve seams.

Follow the graph on page 35 to complete the front and back of the jumper. Follow the chart opposite for the sleeves, incorporating the lower floral motifs into the left sleeve and the upper floral motif into the right sleeve, but continue the trellis throughout as indicated by the dotted red lines and as described above. The key for the charts is given below.

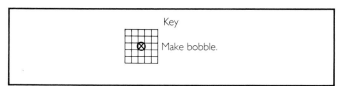

Key

⊗ Make bobble.

Gibraltar

Collectors call the "Gibraltar" colours 'ice cream colours' and you can see why! Clarice Cliff's unusual choice of colours makes this straight-forward seascape something special. Unfortunately, this delightful colour scheme was only utilised on a couple of other designs, including "Pink Roof Cottage", which is quite rare. "Gibraltar" was introduced in 1931 and was produced until 1933. The design appeared on a number of Cliff's pottery shapes and here it is shown on an octagonal plate, sugar dredger and vase.

The chalky pastels in this popular seascape design inspired this crisp, long-line, summer knit. Work the border using the intarsia method.

BACK
Using 3¼mm needles and white, cast on 98 sts and work in k2, p2 rib for 7½cm, inc 20 sts evenly across last row of rib (118 sts).

Change to 4mm needles and work rows 1–183 from chart in st st.

Shape neck: keeping chart correct, work 46 sts, and turn, work on these sts for first side. Dec 1 st at neck edge on next 6 rows, cont straight until row 190 has been worked. Cast off all sts. Slip centre 26 sts on a holder for neckband, rejoin yarn to remaining sts and, keeping chart pattern correct, work decreases to match first side. When row 190 is complete, cast off remaining 40 sts.

MATERIALS
Melinda Coss DK cotton –
white: 600gm; mid-blue:
150gm; pink: 150gm; yellow:
150gm; apple green: 50gm.

NEEDLES
One pair of 3¼mm and one
pair of 4mm needles. Two
stitch holders.

TENSION
Using 4mm needles and
measured over st st, 20 sts and
28 rows = 10cm square.

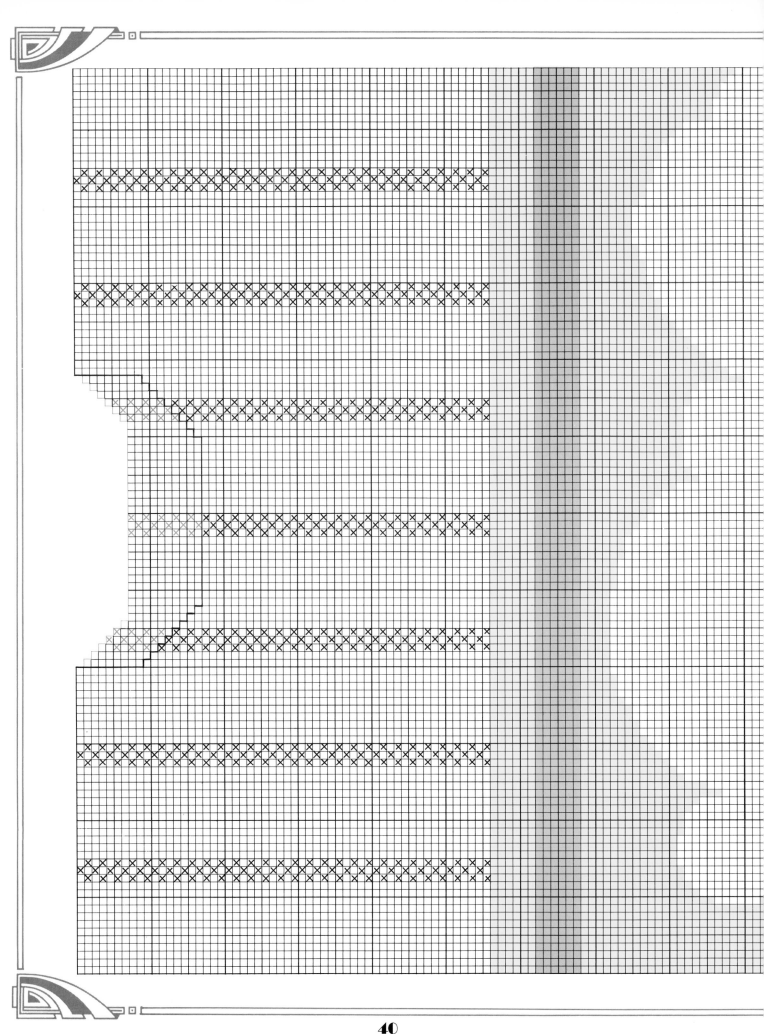

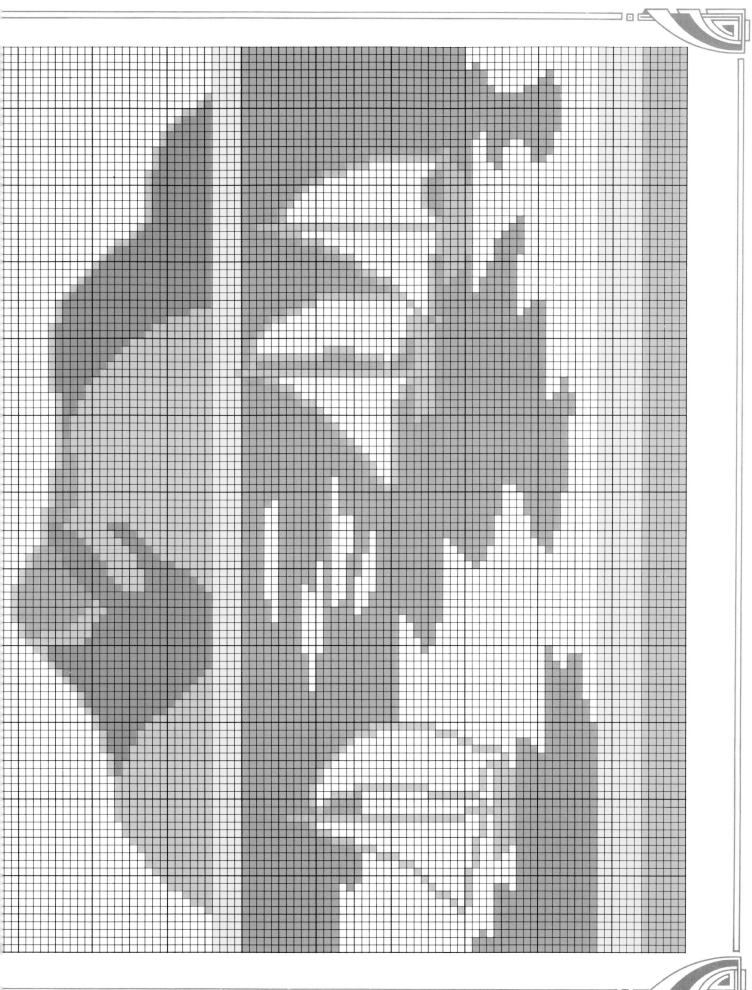

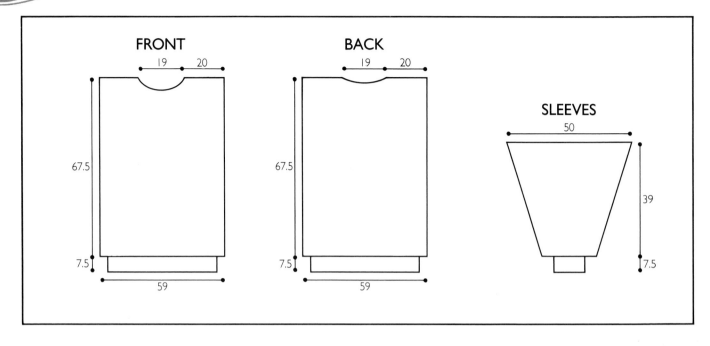

FRONT — 19 — 20 — 67.5 — 7.5 — 59

BACK — 19 — 20 — 67.5 — 7.5 — 59

SLEEVES — 50 — 39 — 7.5

FRONT

Work as for back until row 173 from chart has been completed.

Shape neck: next row: work 48 sts, turn, cont on these sts for first side. Dec 1 st at neck edge on every row until 40 sts remain, then cont until row 190 has been worked. Cast off all sts. Slip centre 22 sts onto a holder for neckband, rejoin yarn to remaining sts and, keeping chart correct, work decreases to match first side. When row 190 is complete, cast off remaining 40 sts.

SLEEVES (both alike)

Using 3¼mm needles and white, cast on 48 sts and work in k2, p2 rib for 7½cm, inc 10 sts evenly across last row (58 sts).

Change to 4mm needles and work from sleeve chart, inc 1 st at each end of every 5th row until you have 100 sts. Cont straight until chart is complete, cast off loosely.

NECKBAND

Join left shoulder seam. Using 3¼mm needles, white, and with RS facing, pick up and knit 15 sts down left front neck, 22 sts held for centre front, 15 sts up right front neck, 7 sts down right back neck, 26 sts held for centre back, 7 sts up left back neck (92 sts). Work in k2, p2 rib for 6 rows. Cast off ribwise.

MAKING UP

Using flat seams throughout, join right shoulder and neckband seams. Set sleeves into place. Join sleeve and side seams.

Follow the chart on pages 40–1 to complete the back and front. The chart opposite should be followed to complete the sleeves. The key for the charts is given below.

> Key
>
> X Purl on a knit row and knit on a purl row in base colour.

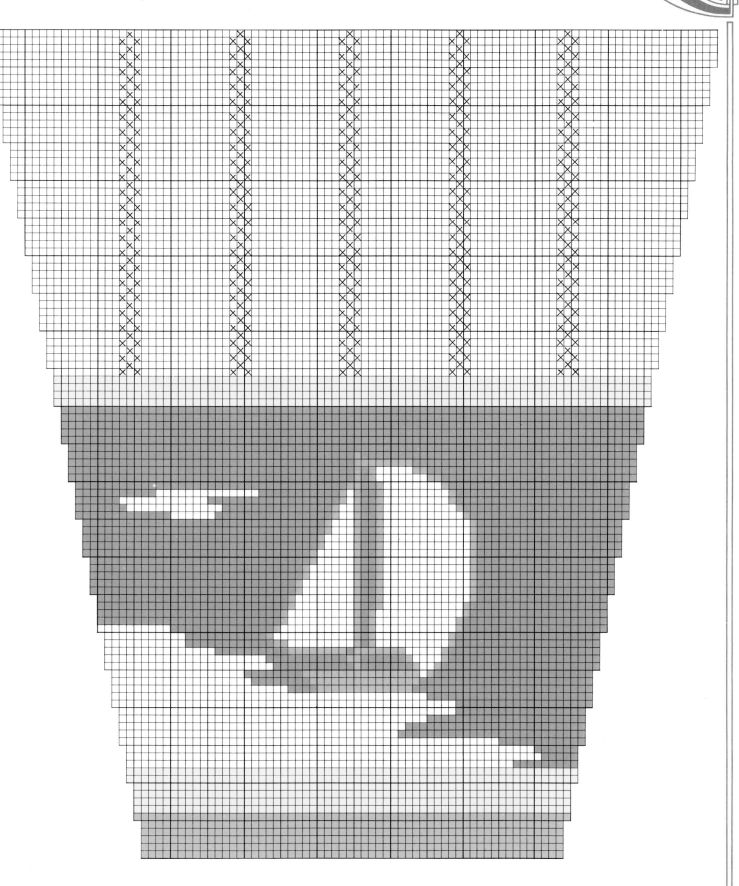

Autumn

The "Autumn" design was one of Clarice Cliff's classic 'cottage in a landscape' themes. It is one of her most flowing landscapes, the sinuous trees and cloud-shaped bushes are very natural. "Autumn" was produced from 1931 to 1933, but many customers ordered 'matchings' right up to the end of 1939. Its success is proven by the vast number of colourways it was produced in, including "Pastel Autumn" (1932) and "Autumn Orange" (1933), but the most popular colourway was "Autumn Blue". The illustration shows examples of "Autumn Red" (wall plaque), "Autumn Blue" (vase) and "Autumn Green" (teapot).

This aran-weight cropped jacket is loosely based on the design called "Autumn".

BACK
Using 4½mm needles and beige, cast on 86 sts. K1, p1 rib for 4 rows. Change to 5½mm needles and commence following chart for back in st st. Work straight to shoulder shaping. Cast off 10 sts at beg of next 4 rows and 9 sts at beg of following 2 rows. Cast off remaining 28 sts.

RIGHT FRONT
Using 4½mm needles and beige, cast on 40 sts. Work in k1, p1 rib for 4 rows. Change to 5½mm needles and, working in st st, follow chart for right front to neck shaping. Next row (RS): cast off 6 sts at beg of this row, then cast off 1 st at neck edge on the 5 following 3rd rows. Work straight to shoulder shaping. Next row (WS): **shape shoulders:** cast off 10 sts at beg of this row and the following alt row. Work 1 row. Cast off remaining 9 sts.

LEFT FRONT
Work as for right front following left front chart and reversing shapings.

MATERIALS
Melinda Coss aran wool – beige: 350gm; black, red tweed, green tweed, royal blue, gold, fuchsia, white: 50gm of each. 5 toggles.

NEEDLES
One pair of 4½mm and one pair of 5½mm needles.

TENSION
Using 5½mm needles and measured over st st, 16 sts and 24 rows = 10cm square.

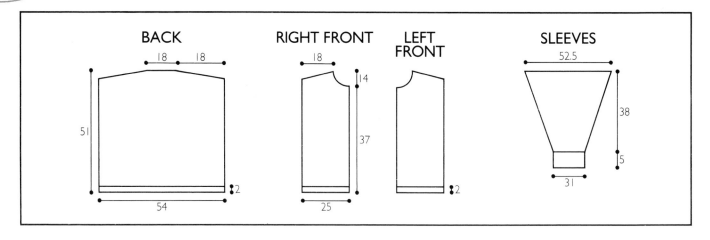

BACK

18 18

51

54

2

RIGHT FRONT

18

14

37

25

2

LEFT FRONT

2

SLEEVES

52.5

38

5

31

LEFT SLEEVE

Using 4½mm needles and beige, cast on 50 sts. Work in k1, p1 rib for 12 rows. Change to 5½mm needles and, working in st st, follow the chart, inc 1 st at each end of every 5th row until you have 84 sts. Cont straight until chart is complete. Cast off loosely.

RIGHT SLEEVE

Work as for left sleeve, knitting stripe after cuff but omitting blue area at the top of the chart.

BUTTONBAND

Using 4½mm needles and beige, cast on 9 sts. K1, p1 rib until band reaches beg of the neck shaping when slightly stretched. Place 5 pins evenly up band with first pin 4 rows from the bottom and last pin 3 rows from the top.

BUTTONHOLE BAND

Work as for buttonband, making buttonholes to correspond with positions of pins as follows. First buttonhole row: rib 4, cast off 2, rib 3. On return row, cast on 2 sts over those cast off on previous row.

NECKBAND

Using a flat seam, join shoulders and stitch buttonband and buttonhole band into position. Using 4½mm needles and beige, pick up 9 sts from buttonhole band, 32 sts up right side, 32 sts across back and 32 sts down left side, and 9 sts from buttonband. K1, p1 rib for 4 rows. Cast off.

MAKING UP

Using a flat seam, join sleeves to body, then join sleeve and side seams. Sew toggles into position.

Follow the chart on page 48 to complete the back and the charts opposite to complete the fronts of the jacket. To complete the sleeves follow the chart on page 49, but omit the blue area at the top of the chart when knitting the right sleeve as described above.

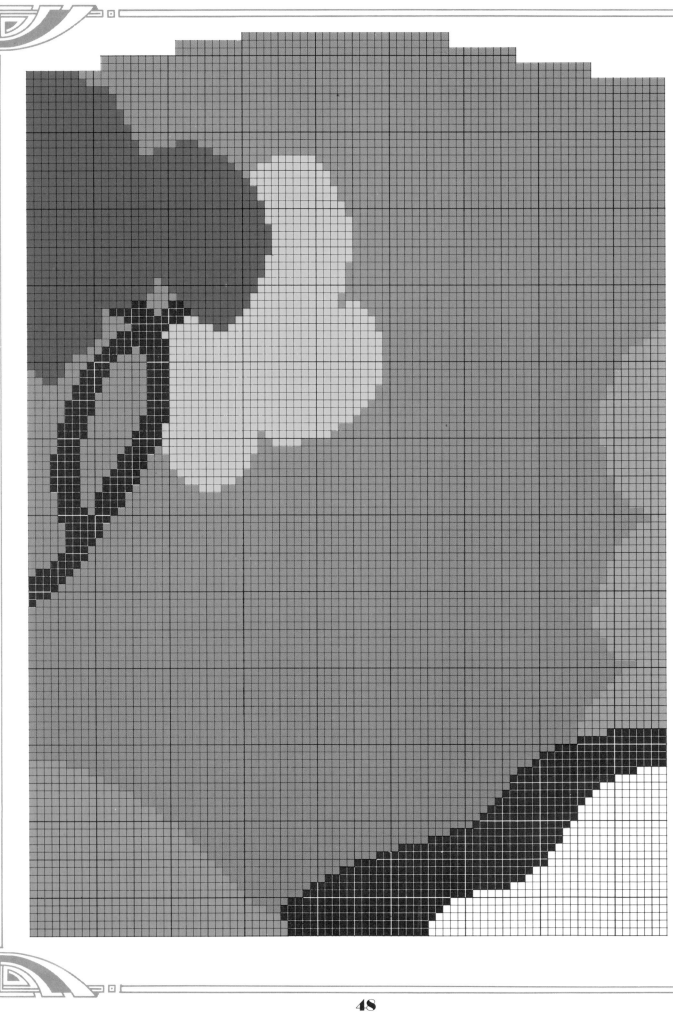

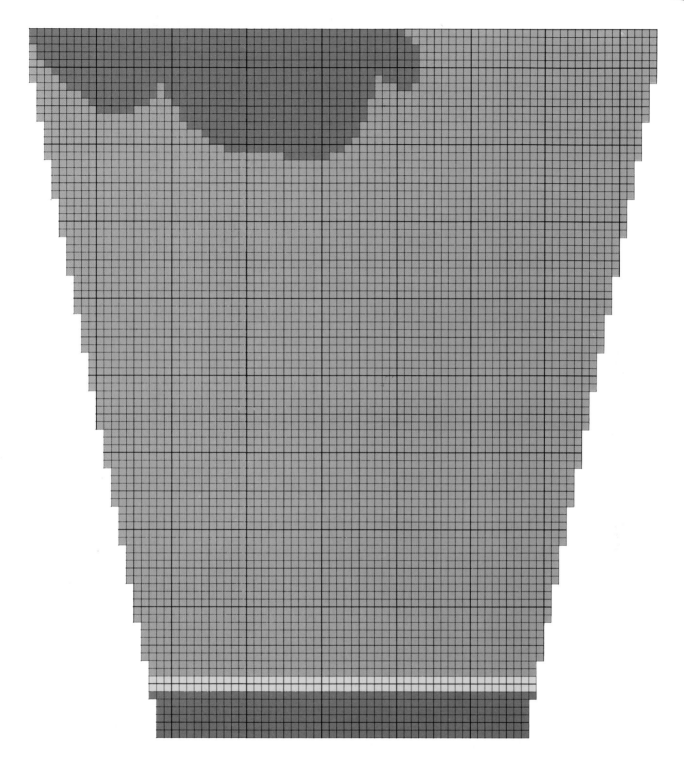

Sunburst

The 1928 original "Bizarre" designs in rust red, browns, blues and yellows, led to slightly more sophisticated geometric patterns by 1930, this is when "Sunburst" was issued. Here the design is seen on a vase. The paintresses had learned to apply colours in a more subtle manner and Clarice Cliff started to use what collectors call coloursets, for instance the red, orange, yellow and brown colour scheme of this design was to reappear on the 1931 "House and Bridge" design.

The bold geometric pattern easily adapts into a graphic 'sloppy Joe' for him or her. It is worked in aran-weight wool using the intarsia method.

BACK
Using 3¼mm needles and peat, cast on 90/108 sts and work in k1, p1 rib for 25 rows, inc 26/24 sts evenly across last row of rib (116/132 sts).
Change to 4½mm needles and work in st st following the chart until 90/94 rows are complete. **Shape armholes:** cast off 5/5 sts at beg of the next 2 rows. Cont working from chart, ignoring the neck shapings until row 150/155 is complete. **Shape shoulders:** cast off 17/21 sts at beg of next 2 rows, then 17/20 sts at beg of next 2 rows. Leave remaining 38/40 sts on a holder for turtle neck.

FRONT
Work as for back until row 128/135 has been completed. **Shape neck:** 1st size (RS): work 44 sts from chart and turn. Work on these sts for first side as follows: keeping chart correct, cast off 4 sts at neck edge on next row, work 1 row, cast off 3 sts at neck edge on next row, work 1 row. Cast off 2 sts at neck edge on next row, work 1 row, cast off 1 st at neck edge on next row. Cont from chart until row 150 has been completed. **Shape shoulder:** cast off 17 sts at beg of the next row, work 1 row, cast off remaining sts. Slip centre 18 sts onto a holder for turtle neck, rejoin yarn to remaining sts and, keeping chart correct, work to match first side.
2nd size (WS): work 53 sts from chart and turn. Work on these sts for first side, cast off 4 sts at neck edge on next row. Work 1 row, cast off 3 sts at neck edge at beg of next row. Work 1 row, cast off 2 sts at neck edge at beg of next and following alt row. Work 1 row, cast off 1 st at neck edge at beg of the next row. Cont on remaining sts until row 155 from chart has been worked.
Shape shoulder: cast off 21 sts at beg of next row, work 1 row, cast off remaining sts. Slip centre 16 sts onto a holder for turtle neck, rejoin yarn to

---

MATERIALS
Melinda Coss aran-weight wool – peat: 300gm; scarlet: 200gm; tan: 150gm; white: 150gm; gold: 100gm; brick: 100gm.

NEEDLES
One pair of 3¼mm and one pair of 4½mm needles. Two stitch holders.

TENSION
Using 4½mm needles and measured over st st, 18 sts and 25 rows = 10cm square. Ribs worked on 3¼mm needles.

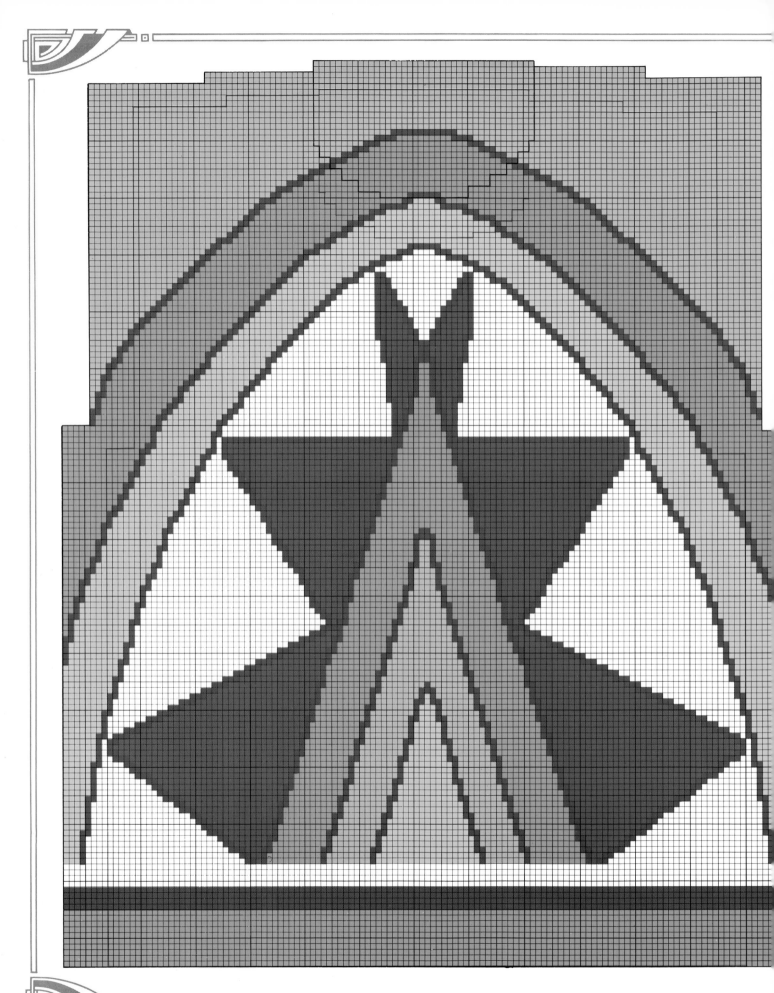

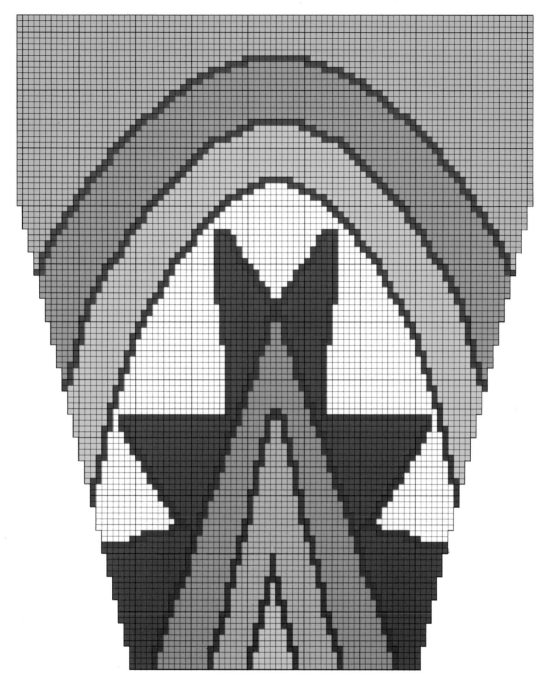

Follow the chart opposite to complete the back and front of the jumper. The chart above should be followed to complete the sleeves.

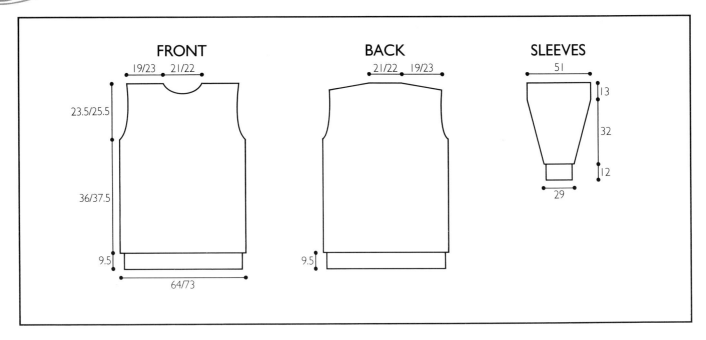

remaining sts and, keeping chart correct, work to match first side.

SLEEVES

Using 3¼mm needles and peat, cast on 48 sts. Work in k1, p1 rib for 30 rows, inc 4 sts evenly across last row of rib (52 sts). Change to 4½mm needles and work in st st from the chart, inc 1 st at each end of every 4th row until you have 92 sts. Cont straight from chart until row 113 has been worked. Cast off loosely.

TURTLE NECK

Join right shoulder seam. Using 3¼mm needles and peat and with RS facing, pick up and knit approx 26/32 sts down left front neck, 18/16 sts across centre front, approx 26/32 sts up right front neck, and 38/40 sts across back neck. Working in k, inc 20 sts evenly across first row (128/140 sts). Work in k1, p1 rib for 8cm. Change to 4½mm needles and work in k1, p1 rib for 12cm. Cast off loosely ribwise.

MAKING UP

Join left shoulder and turtle neck seams. Set sleeves into place, joining centre of sleeve to shoulder seam and the rest set evenly each side to armhole shapings. Sew last 5 rows from sleeve to armhole. Cast off sts. Join remainder of sleeve seams and side seams.

Latona Red Roses

"Latona" was the name of a glaze, not a design, issued with a variety of floral patterns from late 1929 onwards. "Red Roses" was issued in 1930 and was produced by a decorator outlining the design in indian ink, the red and black colours were then filled in and when the piece was fired the lines fired off. This is why the design has a stencil effect. The illustration shows two gigantic 18in (45cm) high "Yo-Yo" vases decorated in "Latona Red Roses", beside them is a standard size "Yo-Yo" vase, 9in (23cm) tall, in the "Blue Firs" design.

This slick waistcoat is worked using the fairisle method in double-knitting wool. The pattern comes in two sizes.

LEFT FRONT

Using 4mm needles and white, cast on 3 sts. P 1 row while beginning to follow chart. Use separate balls for each rose. Work leaves using separate balls.
Row 1: k1, (m1, k1) twice (5 sts).
Row 2: p.
Rows 3–12: work 10 rows in st st, casting on 2 sts at

the end of every row (25 sts).
Row 13: k to end; cast on 2 sts.
Row 14: p to end; cast on 3 sts.
Rows 15 and 16: work as rows 13 and 14 (35 sts).
Row 17: work as row 13.
Row 18: p to end; cast on 5/6 sts.
Rows 19–22: rep rows 17 and 18 twice more (56/59 sts). Mark this point as level of cast-on edge for back.**
Next row (RS): work 14 rows straight in st st.
Next row: k2, m1, k to end.
Next row (WS): work 6 rows in st st.
Next row: k2, m1, k to end. Work 7 rows. Cont in st

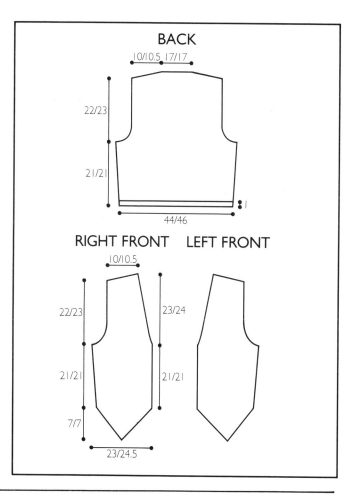

BACK

10/10.5 17/17

22/23

21/21

44/46

RIGHT FRONT   LEFT FRONT

10/10.5

22/23   23/24

21/21   21/21

7/7

23/24.5

MATERIALS
Melinda Coss DK wool –
black: 200gm; white: 100gm;
red: 50gm. 4 buttons 1cm in
diameter.

NEEDLES
One pair of 3¼mm and one
pair of 4mm needles.

TENSION
Using 4mm needles and
measured over st st, 24 sts and
32 rows = 10cm square.

st, making 1 st as before for side shaping on next row and on every following 8th row until you have 63/66 sts. Work straight, following chart to armhole shaping.

Next row (RS): cast off 5/6 sts, k until 2 sts remain, k2 tog.

Next row: p 57/59 sts. Dec 1 st at neck edge on every k row. *At the same time*, dec 1 st at side edge on next 7/8 rows and on following 3 alt rows. Then keep side edge straight and cont to dec as before for neck shaping until 29/30 sts remain. Dec 1 st at neck edge every 4th row until 24/25 sts remain. Work straight to shoulder shaping. **Shape shoulders:** cast off 8 sts at beg of next row and the following alt row. Cast off 8/9 sts at beg of the next alt row.

RIGHT FRONT

Work as for left front, reversing shapings – i.e., chart shaping represents WS of work.

BACK

Using black and 3¼mm needles, cast on 96/102 sts. Work 2 rows in k1, p1 rib. Row 3: k16/19, (k twice in next st, k6) 10 times, k10/13 (106/112 sts).

Change to 4mm needles and work in moss st – i.e., row 1: k1, p1 to end. Row 2: p1, k1 to end for 11 rows. Next row: cont in moss st, *inc 1, moss st to end, inc 1.* Work in moss st for 6 rows, then rep from * to *. Work in moss st for 7 rows. Cont in moss st, making 1 st at each end as set on next row and the 4 following 8th rows.

Work straight on these 120/126 sts for 4 rows. **Shape armholes:** cast off 5/6 sts at beg of next 2 rows. Dec 1 st at both ends of next 7/8 rows and of following 3 alt rows. Work straight on remaining 90/92 sts until back matches fronts to shoulder shaping. **Shape shoulders:** cast off 8 sts at beg of next 4 rows and 8/9 sts at beg of following 2 rows. Cast off remaining 42/42 sts. **Join shoulder seams and side seams.**

LEFT BAND

Using 3¼mm needles and black, cast on 6 sts. Work in moss st until the band fits from the centre back neck to the point where the bottom shaping begins. **Mitre the corner:** next row: work in moss st to last 2 sts, turn, moss st to end. Next row: moss st to last 4 sts, turn, moss st to end. Next row: rep last row. Next row: moss st to end. Cont in moss st to the tip of the point, then work another mitre. Cont straight until band is 1cm short of reaching side seam. Dec 1 st at outer edge on every row until 2 sts remain. K2 tog, fasten off.

RIGHT BAND

Using pins, mark 4 button positions on left band. Work as for left band, reversing directions in which mitres are worked and making buttonholes to correspond with position of pins as follows: moss st 2, cast off 2, moss st 2. Next row: cast on 2 sts over those cast off on previous row.

ARMBANDS

Using 3¼mm needles and black, cast on 6 sts and work in moss st until band is long enough to reach around the armhole when slightly stretched.

MAKING UP

Using flat seams throughout, stitch left and right bands and armbands neatly into position taking care that mitres fit neatly around the shaped corners. Sew on buttons as indicated by pins.

Follow this chart for the left and right fronts.

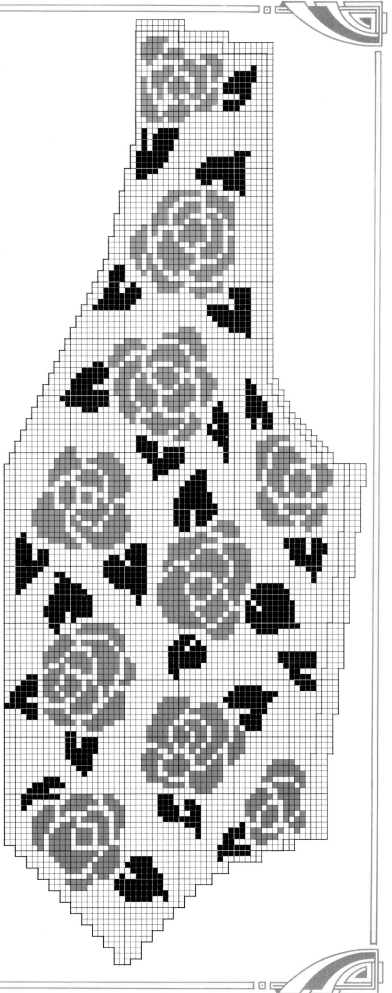

Melon

Introduced in 1930, "Melon" was a good selling design for nearly three years. The pieces shown here are all in the most popular colourway, but variations were produced with the dominant colour being green, orange or red. Clarice Cliff had a definite personal preference for designs such as "Melon", as witnessed by her comments during an interview in London in 1931. 'I have always loved vivid bright colours, and think the modern idea of using these for pottery adds such a cheerful note to our tables and to our rooms. The more or less stereotyped and tame designs that preceded them were, after all rather drab, and lacking in interest. I love mixing bold tints – rich oranges, reds, greens, blues and mauves. These make a glorious riot of colour on large articles of pottery.'

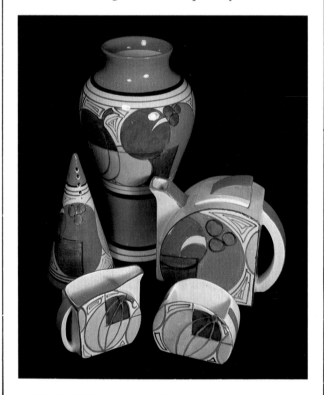

This V-neck, self-striped sweater has a fairisle border in the "Melon" design. Instructions are given for two sizes.

BACK
Using 3¼mm needles and purple, cast on 138 sts and work in k2, p2 rib for 2½cm.
Change to 4mm needles and work in self-stripe pattern as follows:
Row 1 (RS): p7, *C2L (k 2nd st behind first st, then k first st, slipping both sts off needle together), p13. Rep from * to last 11 sts, C2L, p9.
Row 2: k9, p2, *k13, p2, rep from * to last 7 sts, k7.
These 2 rows form the self-stripe pattern. Cont in pattern for 5cm. Now working in st st (knit side is RS), work 40 rows from chart. Then with sts as set after rib, rep 2 rows of self-stripe in pattern until work measures 77½cm from cast-on edge. **Shape shoulders:** keeping pattern correct, cast off 11 sts at beg of the next 6 rows, then 14 sts at beg of next 2 rows. Leave remaining 44 sts on a holder for neckband.

FRONT
Work as for back until work measures 49½cm, ending with a WS row. **Shape V-neck:** keeping pattern correct, work 69 sts and turn, work on these sts for first side, dec 1 st at V edge on next and every following 4th row until 47 sts remain.
Cont in pattern until work measures same as back to shoulder, ending with a WS row. **Shape shoulder:** keeping pattern correct, cast off 11 sts at beg of next and 2 following alt rows. Work 1 row, cast off remaining sts. Rejoin yarn to remaining sts and complete to match first side.

SLEEVES
Using 3¼mm needles and purple, cast on 50/56 sts and work in k2, p2 rib for 14cm inc 13 sts evenly across last row (63/69 sts).
Change to 4mm needles and work 4 rows in st st in rust, inc 1 st at each end of last row. Now work in

---

MATERIALS
Melinda Coss DK wool – purple: 550gm; contrast colours to match graph: less than 50gm of each.

NEEDLES
One pair of 3¼mm and one pair of 4mm needles. One stitch holder.

TENSION
Using 4mm needles and measured over st st, 24 sts and 32 rows = 10cm square.

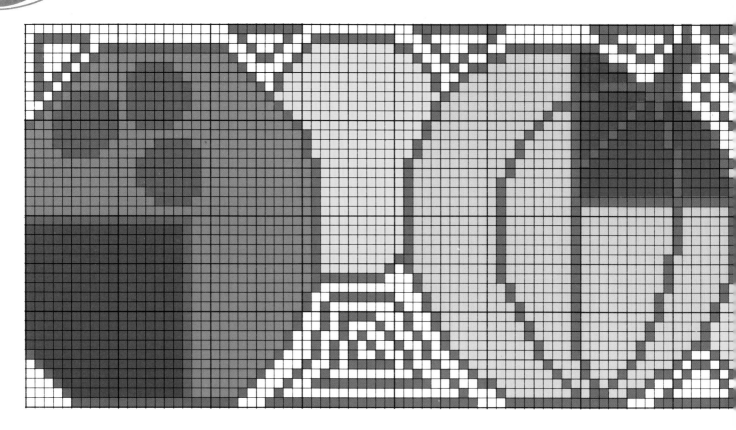

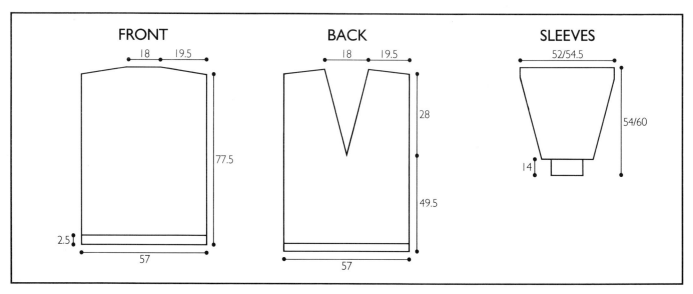

FRONT

18   19.5

77.5

2.5

57

BACK

18   19.5

28

49.5

57

SLEEVES

52/54.5

54/60

14

self-stripe pattern as for back, setting sts as follows:
Next row: p9/12, (C2L, p13) 3 times, C2L, p9/12.
With sts thus set cont in pattern, inc 1 st at each end
of every following 4th row until there are 125/119 sts,
then for second size only at each end of every 5th
row until there are 131 sts. *At the same time*, when
you have 15 sts in purl at each end of row, start
another C2L stripe. After last inc, cont in pattern
until work measures 54/60cm. Cast off all sts.

NECKBAND
Join left shoulder seam. Using 3¼mm needles,
purple and with RS facing, pick up and knit approx
88 sts down left front neck, 1 st across centre front,
approx 88 sts up right front neck and 44 sts across
back neck (221 sts). Starting with a purl row and
using rust, work 4 rows in st st, dec 1 st each side of
centre front st on every row. Break off rust and cont
in purple in k2, p2 rib (dec each side of centre front st

60

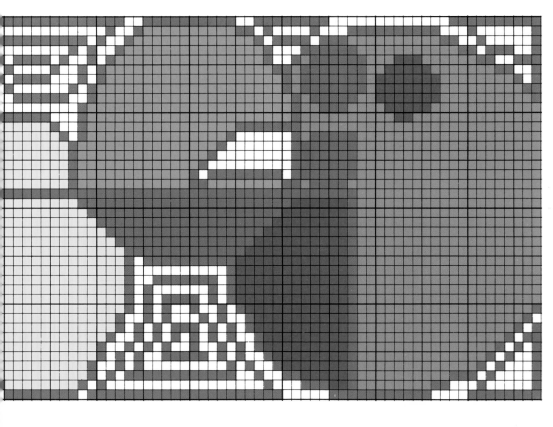

This chart should be incorporated into the back and front of the sweater as described on page 58.

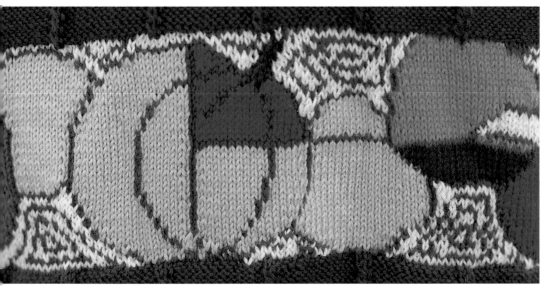

as before) until neckband depth is 2½cm. Cast off in rib, dec 1 st each side of centre front st as you do so.

MAKING UP
Join right shoulder and neckband seams. Set sleeves and sew into place. Join side and sleeve seams.

Da Silva Bruhn Man's Sweater

The original name Clarice Cliff gave "Carpet" is not known but we do know that she copied it from an Ivan Da Silva Bruhn carpet design she saw in a French magazine, *Mobilier et Décoration*, hence the choice of attributed name. "Carpet" was produced mainly in 1930 and in two colourways, red or orange; both are quite rare. The fact that this set is so carefully painted, and in red, a colour used less and less as the "Bizarre" shop majored on orange more and more, indicates that it was probably ordered by a customer as a one-off. It dates from late 1931, a year after the design appeared.

This man's aran-weight crew-neck sweater is simple to work in stocking stitch using the intarsia method.

FRONT

Using 6mm needles and red, cast on 100 sts.
Row 1: k2 red, p2 ecru, rep to end.
Row 2: k2 ecru, p2 red, rep to end.
Rep these 2 rows until rib measures 7cm. Change to ecru and begin following the chart in st st to **front neck shaping**. Next row: k44, slip remaining 56 sts onto a holder and work on this first set of sts only. Turn, cast off 5 sts, p to end. Dec 1 st at neck edge on next 6 rows (33 sts). Work 3 rows, slip remaining 33 sts onto a stitch holder. Return to sts held for other side of neck, slip first 12 sts onto a stitch holder, rejoin yarn at neck edge, k to end, turn, p to end, turn, cast off 5 sts, k to end, turn. Dec 1 st at neck edge on next 6 rows. Work 2 rows, place remaining sts on a spare needle.

BACK

Work as for front following the chart in st st to **back neck shaping**. K43, slip remaining 57 sts onto a spare needle and work on this first set of 43 sts only, turn, cast off 6 sts, p to end. Dec 1 st at neck edge on next 4 rows. Work 2 rows. Leave remaining 33 sts on a spare needle. Return to sts held for other side of neck. Slip the first 14 sts onto a stitch holder, rejoin yarn to remaining sts, k to end, turn, p to end, turn, cast off 6 sts at beg of next row, then dec 1 st at neck edge on next 4 rows. Work 1 row. Leave sts on a spare needle.

SLEEVES (both alike)

Using 6mm needles and red, cast on 40 sts.
Row 1: k2 red, p2 ecru to end.
Row 2: k2 ecru, p2 red to end.
Rep these 2 rows until work measures 7cm. Change to ecru and cont following sleeve chart in st st, inc 1st at each end of the 4th row and the 6 following 4th rows. Then inc 1 st at each end of the 13 following 5th rows (80 sts). Work 5 rows. Cast off.

NECKBAND

With RS of work together, k left shoulder seam. Turn work back to RS and, with ecru and 5½mm needles, pick up and k 72 sts evenly around the neck to include those held on holders for back and front. K2, p2 rib for 6cm. Cast off. K right shoulder seams together, turn neckband inwards and slip stitch cast-off edge to pick-up edge.

MAKING UP

Using a flat seam, join sleeves to jumper; join sleeve and side seams.

MATERIALS	NEEDLES	TENSION
Melinda Coss aran wool – ecru: 500gm; red: 150gm; black and silver: 50gm of each.	One pair of 5½mm and one pair of 6mm needles. Two stitch holders.	Using 6mm needles and measured over st st, 16 sts and 20 rows = 10cm square.

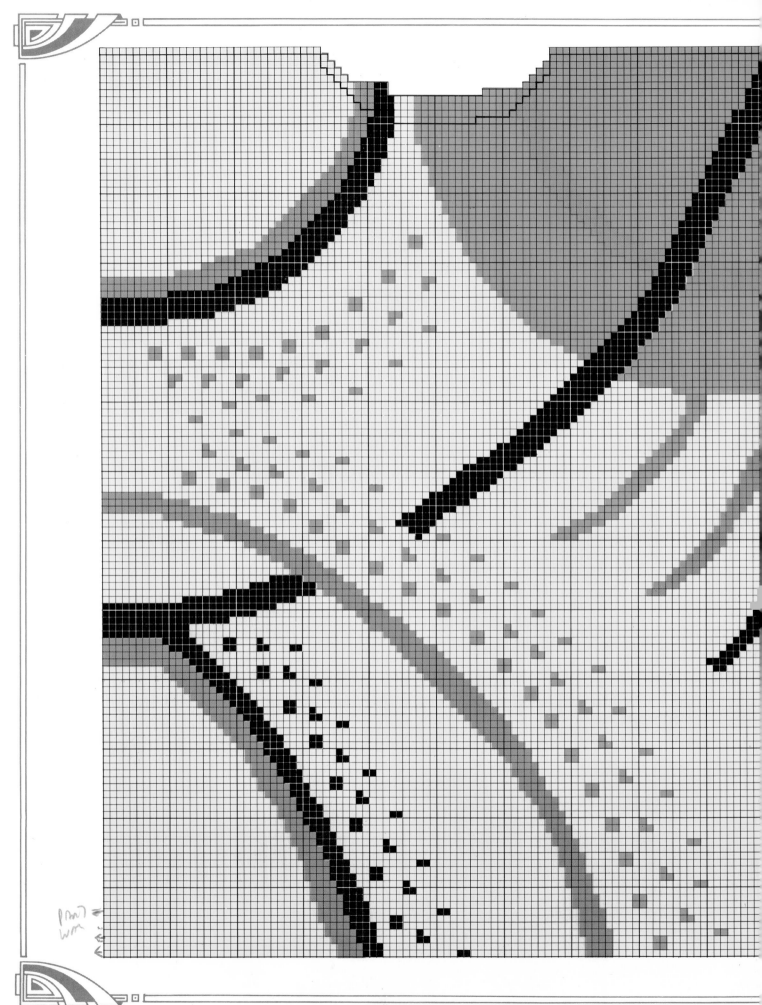

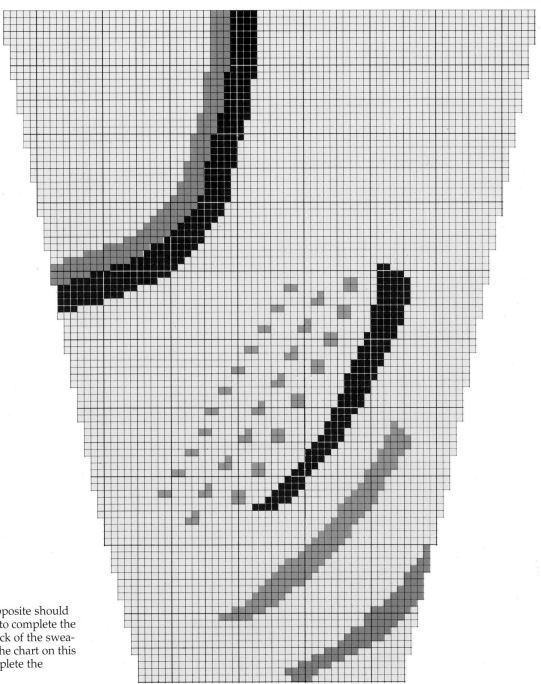

The chart opposite should be followed to complete the front and back of the swea-ter. Follow the chart on this page to complete the sleeves.

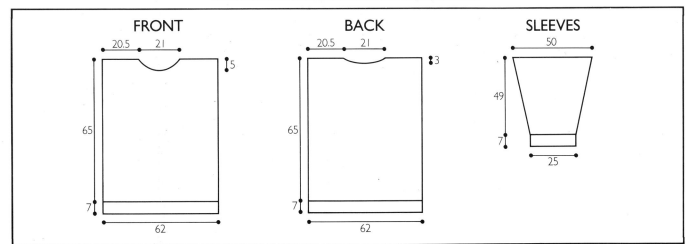

V-Necked Cardigan with Whisper Border

Clarice Cliff developed variations on the original ''Bizarre'' theme, combining flowing lines with geometric shapes. ''Whisper'' is the assumed title of one of these patterns; the true name is not known. The pattern was introduced in 1929.

This bright cable cardigan comes in two sizes and is based on a very early abstract design. The border is worked using the intarsia method.

BACK

Using 3¼mm needles and mauve, cast on 136 sts and work as follows:

Row 1: k1, (p1, k1) 9 times in M. *P2, k6, p2 in T. P2, k6, p2 in A. K1, (p1, k1) 9 times in M. Rep from * to end.

Row 2: p1, (k1, p1) 9 times in M. *K2, p6, k2 in A. K2, p6, k2 in T. P1, (k1, p1) 9 times in M. Rep from * to end.

Row 3: work as row 1.

Row 4: work as row 2.

Row 5: k1, (p1, k1) 9 times in M. *P2, C6F, p2 in T. P2, C6B, p2 in A. K1, (p1, k1) 9 times in M. Rep from * to end.

Row 6: work as row 2.

Row 7: work as row 1.

Row 8: Work as row 2.

These 8 rows form the cable pattern. Rep 4 times more with colours as set (40 rows), inc 2 sts over centre 2 groups of 19 rib sts on last row (140 sts). Change to 4mm needles and, keeping centre 2 cable panels as set, work rows 1–40 from border chart. Then work as follows:

Row 1: k20 in M. *P2, k6, p2 in T. P2, k6, p2 in A. K20 in M. Rep from * to end.

Row 2: p20 in M. *K2, p6, k2 in A. K2, p6, k2 in T. P20 in M. Rep from * to end.

With sts thus set, work 8 rows in cable pattern working cables on 5th row as before. Cont in st st and cable pattern in correct colours until work measures 73cm, ending with a WS row. **Shape shoulders: N.B.** cast off in correct colours and work centre 2 sts together on each cable to prevent centre splaying out. Cast off 12 sts at beg of the next 8 rows. Cast off remaining sts.

LEFT FRONT

Using 3¼mm needles and M, cast on 69 sts and work in rib and cable pattern as on back, setting sts as follows:

Row 1: (side edge RS): k1, (p1, k1) 9 times in M. P2, k6, p2 in A. P2, k6, p2 in T. K1, (p1, k1) 9 times in M. P2, k6, p2 in A. K1 in A.

Row 2: k1 in A. K2, p6, k2 in A. P1, (k1, p1) 9 times in M. K2, p6, k2 in T. K2, p6, k2 in A. K1, (p1, k1) 9 times in M.

Rows 3 and 4: work as rows 1 and 2.

Row 5: k1, (p1, k1) 9 times in M. P2, C6F, p2 in A. P2, C6B, p2 in T. K1, (p1, k1) 9 times in M. P2, C6F, p2, in A. K1 in A.

Rows 6, 7 and 8: work as rows 2, 1 and 2.

These 8 rows set the cable pattern. Rep 4 times more (40 rows), inc 1 st across first set of rib sts on last row (70 sts).

Change to 4mm needles and work from border chart, keeping cable at front edge as set. When chart has been completed, keep front cable sts correct and work remaining sts in st st in M for 40 rows.

Next row: k20 in M. P2, k6, p2 in A. P2, k6, p2 in T.

MATERIALS
Melinda Coss DK wool – mauve (M): 400gm; orange (A): 150gm; turquoise (T): 150gm; ecru (E): 100gm; yellow (Y): 50gm; black (B): 50gm. 7 buttons 2cm in diameter.

NEEDLES
One pair of 3¼mm and one pair of 4mm needles. One cable needle.

TENSION
Using 4mm needles and measured over st st, 24 sts and 32 rows = 10cm square.

K20 in M. P2, k6, p2 in A.

With sts thus set and working cables as in welt (p2, C6F, p2 in A, p2, C6B, p2 in T), to match those at front edge, cont until work measures 38cm, ending with a WS row. **Shape V-neck:** keeping cables in centre correct and working cable at front edge correct as far as possible, shape front as follows:

Next row: pattern to last 3 sts, k2 tog, k1 in A. **N.B.** when all A sts have been decreased, then work this front edge st in M. Cont in this way, dec 1 st at front edge on every 4th row until you have 48 sts. Cont in pattern until work measures the same as the back to the shoulder, ending with a WS row.

Shape shoulder: cast off 12 sts at beg of next and 2 following alt rows, work 1 row, cast off remaining sts.

RIGHT FRONT

Work as for left front, reversing all shapings and setting cables as follows (RS front edge): A,A,T (so cables match back at shoulder), working centre front edge cable as C6B instead of C6F (this cable is worked in A).

SLEEVES

Using 3¼mm needles, cast on 52/58 sts and work in rib and cable pattern as on back, setting sts as follows:

Row 1: k0/1, (p1, k1) 8/9 times in M. P2, k6, p2 in T. P2, k6, p2 in A. (K1, p1) 8/9 times, k0/1 in M.

With sts thus set, cont until work measures 7cm, inc 6 sts over each group of rib sts on last row (64/70 sts). Change to 4mm needles and work from sleeve chart. Inc 1 st at each end of every 4th row as shown. When chart is complete, cont with centre cables in their correct colours and with remaining sts worked in st st in M, inc 1 st at each end of every 4th row as before until you have 126/120 sts. Then for 2nd size only, inc 1 st at each end of every 5th row until you have 132 sts. Cont straight until work measures 47/53cm. Cast off all sts, working 2 sts tog over centre of cables to prevent them splaying out.

LEFT POCKET

Using 4mm needles and M, cast on 40 sts and work as follows:

Row 1: k10 in M. P2, k6, p2 in T. P2, k6, p2 in A. K10 in M.

Row 2: p10 in M. K2, p6, k2 in A. k2, p6, k2 in T. P10 in M.

Row 3: work as row 1.

Row 4: work as row 2.

Row 5: k10 in M. P2, C6F, p2 in T. P2, C6B, p2 in A. K10 in M.

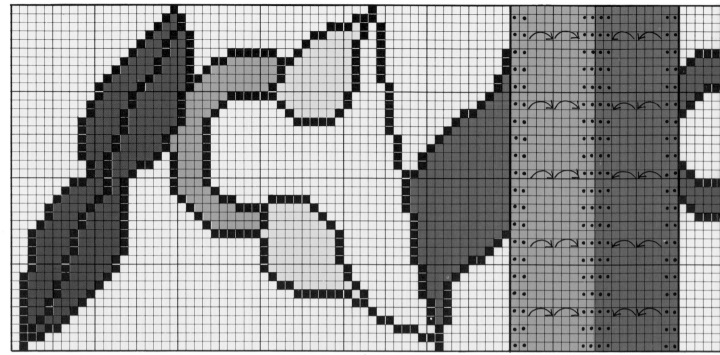

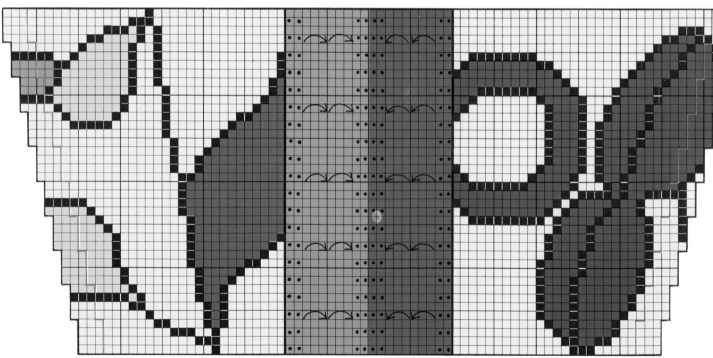

Row 6: work as row 2.
Row 7: work as row 1.
Row 8: work as row 2.
Rep these 8 rows 4 times more (40 rows).
Change to 3¼mm needles and work as follows:
Next row: (p1, k1) 5 times in M. Cable pattern in T.
Cable pattern in A. (K1, p1) 5 times in M.
With sts thus set, work 5 rows more, then cast off in
pattern.

RIGHT POCKET
Work as for left pocket, reversing cable colours so
they match cables on right front of cardigan.

BUTTONBAND
Join shoulder seams. Using 3¼mm needles and M,
cast on 10 sts and work in k1, p1 rib until band fits
neatly up front when slightly stretched, to finish at
centre back neck. Cast off ribwise. Mark positions for

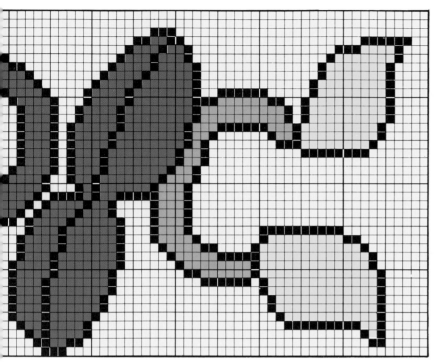

Key

● Purl on right side and knit on wrong side in colour of cable.

⊞ C6F

⊞ C6B

The top chart on pages 68–9 shows the border pattern that should be knitted into the back and front of the cardigan as described on pages 66–7. For the left front work the 70 stitches on the right side of the chart, for the right front work the 70 stitches on the left side of the chart; for both the left and right fronts work the centre cable of the border in orange. The lower chart on page 68 should be incorporated into the sleeves, *see* page 67. The key for the charts is given above.

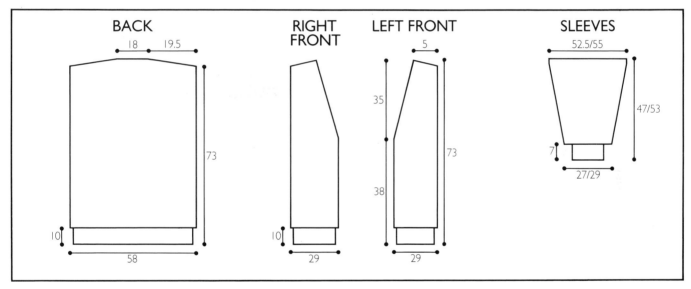

BACK

18 · 19.5

73

10

58

RIGHT FRONT

10

29

LEFT FRONT

5

35

73

38

29

SLEEVES

52.5/55

47/53

7

27/29

7 buttons on this band, the first to come on the 3rd row and the last to come at beg of 'V' shaping with the others spaced evenly between.

BUTTONHOLE BAND

Work as for buttonband, working buttonholes opposite marked positions as follows:
Buttonhole row: rib 4, cast off 2 sts, rib to end.
Next row: rib 4, cast on 2 sts, rib to end.

MAKING UP

Pin buttonband and buttonhole band into place (lady's or man's buttoning, whichever is required), easing to fit and meeting at centre back neck. Sew with flat seam. Sew centre back seam. Set sleeves into place and join to body. Sew side and sleeve seams. Sew on buttons. Pin pockets into place taking care to match cables. Sew on neatly in correct colour.

Crocus

"Crocus" was Clarice Cliff's best selling design. It was introduced late in 1928 and was produced until 1964. Throughout the 1930s new colour variations appeared; "Spring Crocus" in shades of pink, green and yellow; also rarer colourways of all purple, or all blue "Crocus" were produced. Each flower was achieved by three or four brushstrokes, and the leaves were created by a single stroke in the opposite direction. The colourway pictured below on a jug and plate from between 1930 and 1932 is the original "Crocus". Cliff told her 'girls' that the brown was the earth, the yellow the sun!

This fitted lady's jumper with a crocus yoke is worked in double-knitting wool. Use separate balls of yarn for each individual flower but knit the flowers in fairisle.

BACK
Using 3¼mm needles and green, cast on 110 sts. Work 1 row in k1, p1 rib, then change to ginger. Work 20 rows in k1, p1 rib.
Change to 4mm needles. Working in st st throughout, work 2 rows in green, then change to ginger. Work 18 rows in st st, then dec 1 st at each end of next and every following 4th row until you have 90 sts. Work 12 rows straight, then inc on next and every following 4th row until there are 110 sts. Work straight until back measures 47cm (including rib) ending with a WS row. **Shape armholes:** cast off 4 sts at beg of next 2 rows, then dec 1 st at each end of next 5 rows, then 1 st at each end of next 2 alt rows (88 sts). Work 4 rows straight. Change to green, p 1 row. Work in st st for 6 rows in yellow ending on a WS row. Begin following chart in st st, working background in ecru. When chart is complete cast off all stitches.

FRONT
Work as for back to neck shaping. Chart 32 sts, turn, dec 1 st at neck edge on next 4 rows and the following 5 alt rows.
Work straight until row 42 of chart is completed. Cast off remaining 23 sts. Rejoin yarn to remaining sts, cast off 24 sts at centre front, work to end. Shape to match other side of neck.

SLEEVES
Using 3¼mm needles and yellow, cast on 2 sts, k1, p1 rib. Next row: inc 1, rib 2, inc 1. Next row: rib 4. Next row: inc 1 yellow, k1, change to ginger, rib to last st, rib 1 yellow, inc 1 yellow. Next row: rib 2 yellow, rib in ginger to last 2 sts, rib 2 yellow. Rep last 2 rows until you have 50 sts. Work 8cm of rib in ginger throughout.
Change to 4mm needles and inc 1 st at beg and end of next and every following 6th row until you have 80 sts. Cont straight until sleeve measures 46cm from first complete rib row of 50 sts. Begin following chart for sleeve; *at the same time*, work armhole shaping,

MATERIALS
Melinda Coss DK wool – ginger: 350gm; ecru: 85gm; yellow, green, orange, purple, mauve, royal blue and mid-blue: less than 50gm of each.

NEEDLES
One pair of 3¼mm and one pair of 4mm needles.

TENSION
Using 4mm needles and measured over st st, 24 sts and 32 rows = 10cm square.

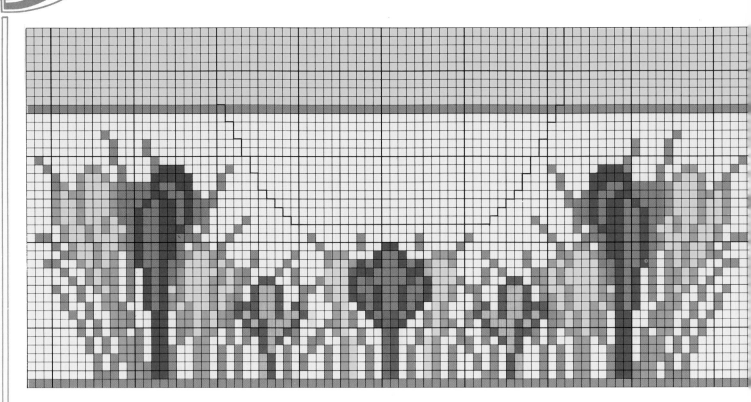

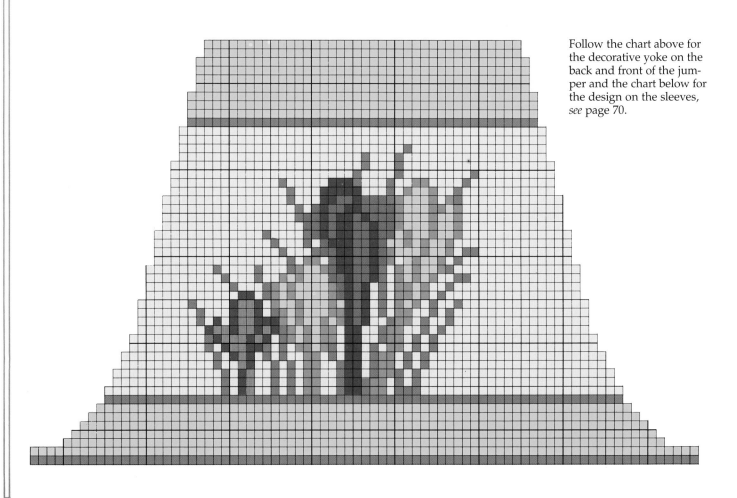

Follow the chart above for the decorative yoke on the back and front of the jumper and the chart below for the design on the sleeves, *see* page 70.

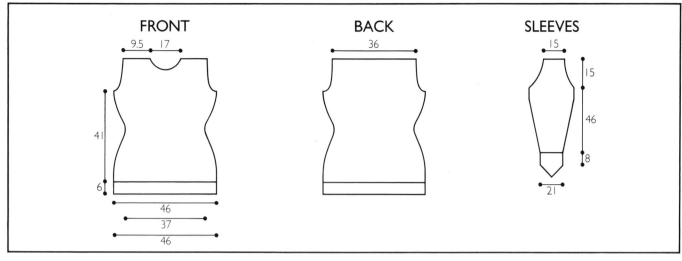

FRONT BACK SLEEVES

beginning with row 2. Cast off 4 sts at beg of this and next row, then 1 st at each end of next 5 rows and following 4 alt rows. Then dec 1 st at each end of the 8 following 4th rows. Work 2 rows straight. Cast off all sts.

COLLAR
Join shoulder seams. Using 3¼mm needles, yellow and with RS facing, k up 28 sts down left front, 24 sts across centre, 28 sts up right front and 42 sts across back neck. Work 4 rows in k1, p1 rib. Work next row

round to middle of centre 24 sts, turn, rib back around to centre front via back, thus keeping front opening. Rib 4, inc 1, rib to last 4 sts, inc 1, rib 4. Rib 3 rows. Rep last 4 rows 3 times. Work 1 row green, cast off in green.

MAKING UP
Sew in sleeves, easing fullness at top. Join side and sleeve seams using a flat seam. Turn down collar and turn back cuffs.

Crocus Hat

This pudding-basin hat is worked in stocking stitch on circular needles using aran-weight wool. The hat is decorated with crocuses that are knitted in 4-ply wool.

HAT
Using a 6mm circular needle and green, cast on 100 sts. K 1 round, p 1 round, k 4 rounds. Change to yellow, k 3 rounds. Change to ecru and a 5mm circular needle and k 8 rounds, dec 4 sts evenly along last round (96 sts). Change to ginger, work 20 rounds. Next round: k2, *k2 tog, k1, rep from * to

last st, k1 (65 sts). K 6 rounds. Next round: k1, k2 tog, rep to last st, k1 (44 sts). K 4 rounds. K2 tog to end (22 sts). K 3 rounds. K2 tog to end (11 sts). Thread yarn back through sts, draw up and secure.

CROCUS PETALS
Using 2¼mm needles and 4-ply, cast on 6 sts in st st. Inc 1 st at each end of every row until you have 14 sts. Work in st st for 8 rows, dec 1 st at each end of every row until you have 4 sts. Cast off. Make 3 petals for each crocus.

MATERIALS
Melinda Coss aran wool – ginger: 50gm; ecru, yellow and green aran, and purple and mid-blue 4-ply: less than 50gm of each. 1m fuse wire. Safety pin.

NEEDLES
One pair of 2¼mm needles; one 5mm (short) and one 6mm (short) circular needle.

TENSION
Using 5mm needles, aran wool and measured over st st, 18 sts and 23 rows = 10cm square.

Take a length of fuse wire long enough to stretch right around a petal leaving approx 4cm free at the bottom. Oversew the fuse wire around the edge of the petal with wool until it can no longer be seen. When you have worked 3 petals in this way, twist all the ends of wire tightly together to form a stem. Wrap green wool tightly around the stem and secure at the top. To make stamens, thread 2 ends of yellow wool through the centre of the crocus and knot the ends. Pin crocus to hat with safety pin.

Banded Gloves Worked on 2 Needles

These gloves are designed to match the crocus hat but by using different colours for the bands you can match up with any of Clarice's designs.

LEFT-HAND GLOVE
Using 2¾mm needles and green, cast on 58 sts. K first row working into the back of every st, then work in k1, p1 rib as follows. Work 3cm in green, 1cm in yellow and 3cm in ecru, ending on a RS row. Change to ginger, p1 row, k1 row, p1 row, cont in ginger and st st. Next row: k27, k twice into next st, k2, k twice into next st, k27, turn, st st 3 rows without shaping. Rep these 4 rows until you have 18 sts between the two sets of 27 sts. **Shape thumb:** k 27 sts, then k 18 sts for thumb, turn, p back 18 sts, turn, k 18 sts. Cast on 3 sts. Work in st st on these 21 sts until thumb measures 5cm, ending on a WS row. **Shape top:** k1, k2 tog, rep to end, p back, k1, k2 tog, rep to end, p back, k2 tog to end of row. Break off yarn, leaving enough to thread back through sts and secure for thumb. With RS facing, rejoin yarn to remaining sts for hand. K 1 row, turn, p back to thumb. Cast on 3 sts and cont knitting across the second set of 27 sts (57 sts). K without shaping for 3½cm.

FIRST FINGER LEFT HAND
With RS of work facing, k 21 sts and slip them onto a thread to be picked up as needed for other fingers. K a further 15 sts for the first finger and slip the remaining 21 sts on another piece of thread. To cont first finger, cast on 3 sts, p back. Work in st st for 6½cm, then shape top as for thumb. Break off wool, leaving an end to thread back. Sew seam.

SECOND FINGER
Pick up 7 sts from the thread on the right side of the first finger and work in st st for 7cm. Shape top as for thumb. Pick up 7 sts from the thread on the left side of the first finger, k7. Cast on 2 sts, turn and p back, cast on 2 sts. Work in st st for 7cm and shape top as before.

THIRD FINGER
Rep as for second finger but knit only 6¾cm before dec for top.

FOURTH FINGER
Work in st st for 5cm the stitches from the right-hand thread, then shape top as before. Pick up sts from the left-hand thread, join in the yarn and cast on 2 sts before knitting first row. Cont knitting in st st for 5cm, then shape top.

RIGHT-HAND GLOVE
Work as for left-hand glove, but add the 2 cast-on sts to the opposite finger pieces.

MAKING UP
Press the hand and fingers as flat as possible. Using flat seams throughout, join the seam of the thumb and the base of the thumb securely. Join the seam down the inside of the first finger. Join the two seams of the second and third fingers, sewing the base of each strongly to the base of the previous finger. Join the inside seam of the fourth finger, and then the outside seam and cont down the outside of the hand to the base of the wrist using correct colours on welts.

MATERIALS
Melinda Coss 4-ply – green: 50gm; ginger: 50gm; ecru and yellow: less than 50gm of each.

NEEDLES
One pair of 2¾mm needles.

TENSION
Using 2¾mm needles and measured over st st, 28 sts and 36 rows = 10cm square.

Four-in-One Jumper

The "Umbrellas and Rain" motif from the "Fantasque" range shows the insides of open umbrellas, and stylised rain. Clarice Cliff's sense of humour produced both a good design and a great name! "Umbrellas and Rain" was introduced late in 1929 and was produced in large quantities for over a year. It was a very good seller. All these pieces – the "Conical" bowl, vase and "Lotus" shape jug – appear to have been decorated by the same outliner.

"Gardenia" was one of Clarice Cliff's best floral patterns. The intricate mesh of leaves and flowers proved popular when it was issued in 1931, and the design was in production for at least a year. There are two colourways, on both the small flowers are blue and lilac, but the large flower can be either red, or orange, the latter being the most common.

This square-necked, long-line jumper can be worked in a choice of four Clarice Cliff designs: "Umbrellas and Rain", "Gardenia", "Gayday" and "Sungay". The written pattern provides the basic instructions for two sizes and the charts show you clearly where to position your selected design. It is worked using the intarsia method.

BACK

Using 3¼mm needles and main colour, cast on 114/126 sts and work in k2, p2 twisted rib for 9cm (k into back of k sts), inc 3/5 sts evenly across last row of rib (117/131 sts).
Change to 4mm needles and commence following the chart in st st, working with any pair of the motifs until you have completed row 138. **Shape armholes:** cast off 8/8 sts at beg of next 2 rows. Work straight to row 206/210. **Shape neck** (RS): k23/30, moss st 55, k23/30. Keeping motifs correct, cont with centre 55 sts worked in moss st until row 214/218 has been completed. Cast off all sts.

FRONT

Work as for back until row 154/158 has been completed. **Neck opening** (RS): k32/39, turn, work on these sts for first side until row 188/192 has been worked. Next row: k to last 9 sts and turn, leave these 9 sts on a holder.
Cont on remaining sts in main colour until graph has been completed. Cast off all sts. Return to remaining sts and slip first 10 of these on a holder for button/buttonhole bands. Work on remaining sts until row 188/192 has been worked. Slip first 36 sts on a stitch holder for neck edge. Now work on remaining sts following chart until it is complete. Cast off all sts.

MATERIALS
Melinda Coss DK wool throughout – **Umbrellas and Rain:** yellow: 800gm; orange: 100gm; remaining colours to match graph: less than 50gm of each.
Gardenia: wine: 800gm; contrast colours to match graph: less than 50gm of each.

Sungay: ecru: 800gm; apple: 100gm; jade: 100gm; royal blue: 100gm; remaining colours to match graph: less than 50gm of each.
Gayday: navy: 800gm; emerald: 100gm; sage: 100gm; wine: 100gm; remaining colours to match graph: less than 50gm of each.
4 buttons 2cm in diameter.

NEEDLES
One pair of 3¼mm and one pair of 4mm needles. Two stitch holders.

TENSION
Using 4mm needles and measured over st st, 24 sts and 32 rows = 10cm square. Ribs worked on 3¼mm needles.

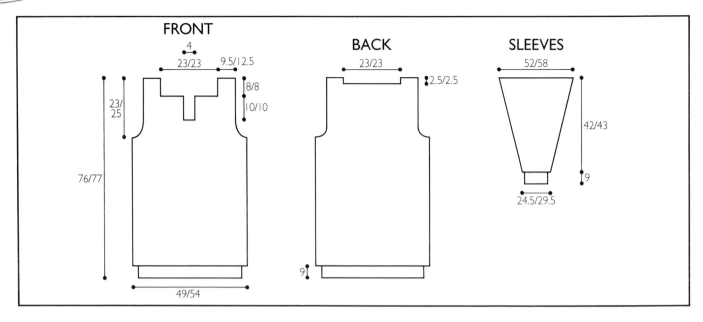

FRONT

4
23/23   9.5/12.5
8/8
10/10
23/25
76/77
49/54

BACK

23/23
2.5/2.5
9

SLEEVES

52/58
42/43
9
24.5/29.5

SLEEVES

Using 3¼mm needles and main colour, cast on 44/48 sts and work in k2, p2 twisted rib for 9cm, inc 15/23 sts evenly across last row of rib (59/71 sts).

Change to 4mm needles and work in st st from chart, inc 1 st at each end of the 2nd row and every following 4th row until you have 125/139 sts. Work 3 rows straight, cast off all sts.

BUTTONHOLE BAND

Using 4mm needles, main colour and with RS facing, pick up and work in moss st on 10 sts on holder for 4 rows. Buttonhole row: moss st 4, cast off 2 sts, moss st to end. Next row: moss st 4, cast on 2 sts, moss st

to end. *Work 10 rows. Rep 2 buttonhole rows. Rep once more from *. Moss st 6 rows. Leave sts on holder.

BUTTONBAND

Using 4mm needles, main colour and with RS facing, working behind buttonhole band sts, pick up same 10 sts again and work in moss st for 34 rows. Leave sts on a holder for neck edge (**N.B.** this band lies behind buttonhole band).

NECK EDGE (Front)

Using 4mm needles, main colour and with RS facing, pick up 9 sts held for left-hand side of neck, 10 sts from buttonband (19 sts) and moss st for 10 rows. Next row: cast off 10 sts from buttonband and work in moss st on remaining sts until band fits neatly up front edge to shoulder. Cast off all sts.

Using 4mm needles, main colour and with RS facing, pick up 10 sts from buttonhole band and remaining sts from front neck edge. Moss st 4 rows, then work 4th buttonhole to match others. Work 2 more rows in moss st. Next row (neck edge): work in moss st on first 9 sts only to match other side to shoulder cast-off row. Cast off these 9 sts. Rejoin yarn to remaining sts and cast off.

MAKING UP

Join shoulder seams. Sew button and buttonhole bands into place along front edges. Sew buttons to match buttonholes. Set sleeves into place, join side and sleeve seams.

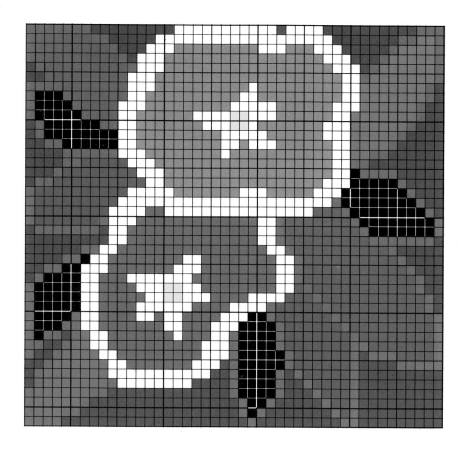

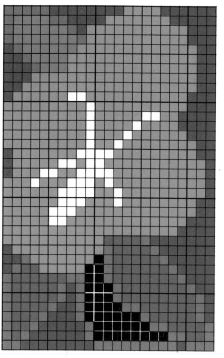

The top charts should be followed for the "Gardenia" motifs and the lower charts for the "Umbrellas and Rain" motifs.

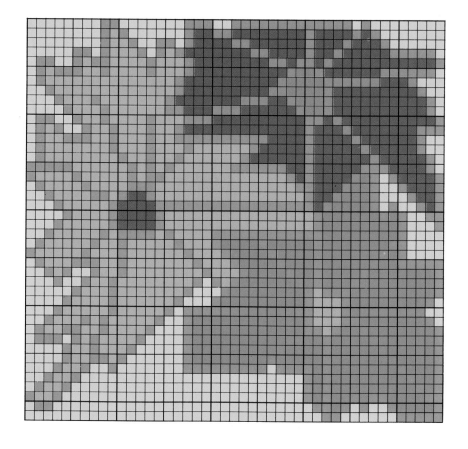

Follow this chart to complete the back and front of the jumper incorporating the chosen motifs in the areas indicated by the red lines.

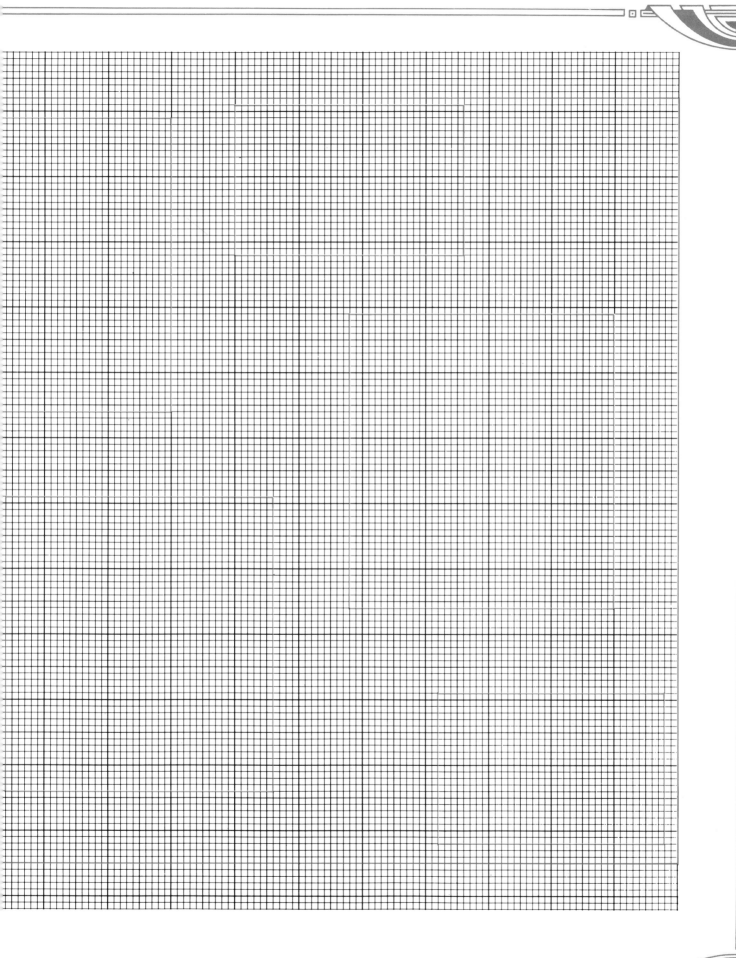

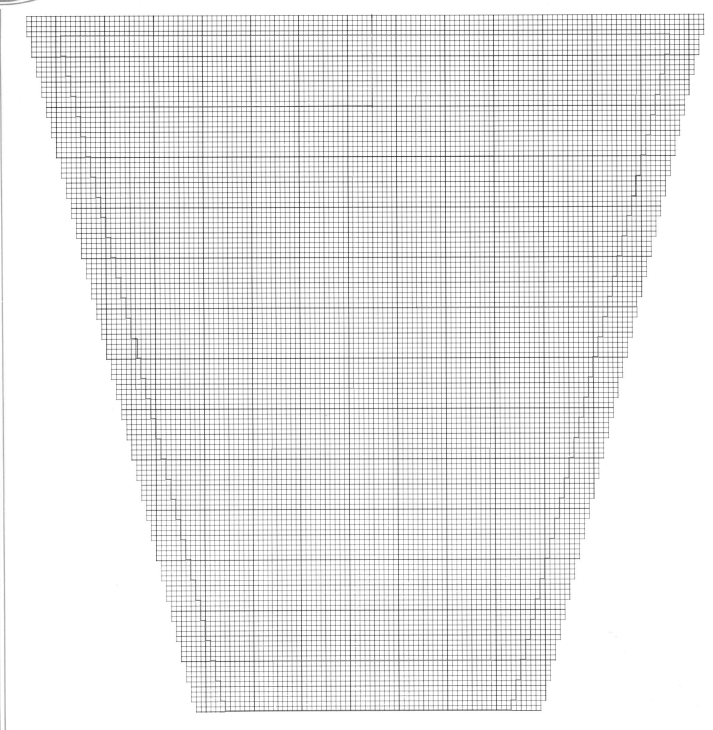

Follow the chart above to complete the sleeves incorporating the chosen motif in the areas indicated by the red lines.

"Gayday" was a follow-up to the extremely successful "Crocus" pattern. It appeared in 1930 and was produced for about five years. "Gayday" has aster flowers in a similar configuration to the "Crocus" design, but this time the banding is brown, yellow and green. Here it is seen on a large "Conical" bowl. Clarice Cliff also issued a colour variation on the "Gayday" theme, but gave it a different name; when the flowers and leaves are green, yellow and blue the design is called "Sungay".

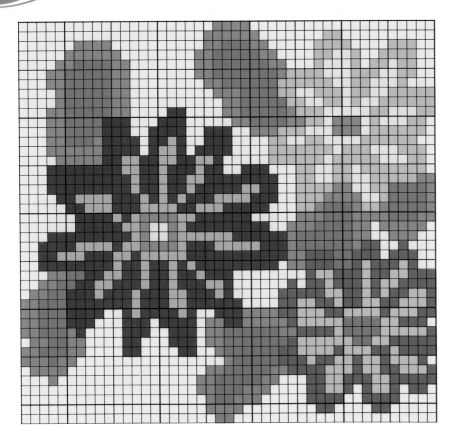

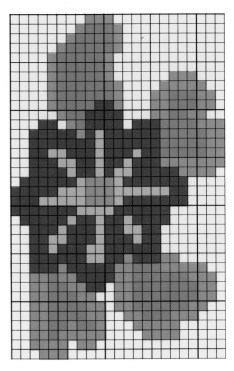

The top charts should be followed for the "Sungay" motifs and the lower charts for the "Gayday" motifs.

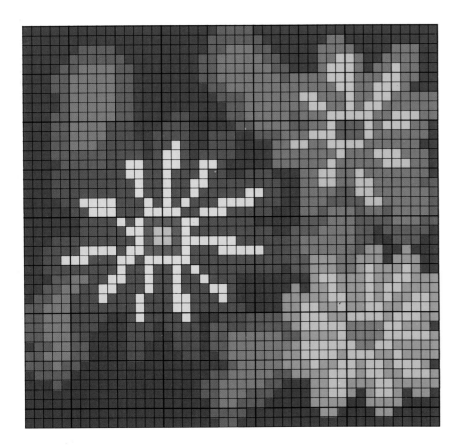

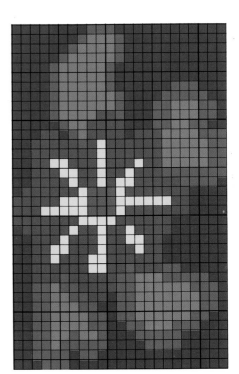

Cubist

Clarice Cliff was influenced by the Cubist school of painting, but she was ahead of general taste, as pieces with Cubist inspired motifs sold poorly. Pictured here on a "Lotus" shape jug is the "Cubist" design, one of the first variations from simple geometrics that Cliff produced. It dates from 1929 and like all early pieces is quite crudely painted.

This aran-weight jacket is loosely based on a cubist design. Worked in stocking stitch using the intarsia method, this jacket is suitable for women and men.

BACK

Using 4mm needles and blue, cast on 90 sts and work in k2, p2 rib for 7cm, inc 14 sts evenly across last row of rib (104 sts).
Change to 5mm needles and work from back chart rows 1–73. **Shape raglans:** keeping chart correct, cast off 2 sts at beg of the next 2 rows.
Row 76: work from chart.
Row 77: work from chart to last 2 sts, k2 tog.
Row 78: work from chart to last 2 sts, p2 tog.
Row 79: work from chart.
Row 80: p2 tog, work from chart to end.
Row 81: k2 tog, work from chart to end.
Keeping chart correct, cont dec as on these 6 rows until row 91 has been worked. Cont to dec at beg of every row until 32 sts remain. Work 2 rows (end of chart). Cast off all sts.

LEFT FRONT

Using 4mm needles and blue, cast on 44 sts and work in k2, p2 rib for 7cm, inc 6 sts evenly across last row of rib (50 sts).
Change to 5mm needles and work rows 1–74 from left front chart. **Shape raglan and front:** keeping chart correct, cast off 2 sts at beg of next row, work 2 rows.
Dec 1 st at front edge on next and every following 6th row 12 times, *at the same time*, dec 1 st on raglan edge on next and every following 3rd row, 6 times in all, then, at this same edge, on every alt row until 2 sts remain. Cont from chart until row 150 has been worked. Fasten off.

RIGHT FRONT

Work rib as for left front. Change to 5mm needles and work rows 1–150 from right front chart working raglan and front shapings as shown on chart. When row 150 has been completed, fasten off.

RIGHT SLEEVE

Using 4mm needles and blue, cast on 40 sts and work in k2, p2 rib for 7cm, inc 4 sts evenly across last row (44 sts).
Change to 5mm needles and work from right sleeve

MATERIALS
Melinda Coss aran-weight wool – blue tweed: 250gm; red: 250gm; yellow: 200gm; black: 150gm; green: 100gm; white: 100gm. 6 buttons 2½cm in diameter.

NEEDLES
One pair of 4mm and one pair of 5mm needles.

TENSION
Using 5mm needles and measured over st st, 18 sts and 23 rows = 10cm square.

Follow this chart to complete the right sleeve of the jacket.

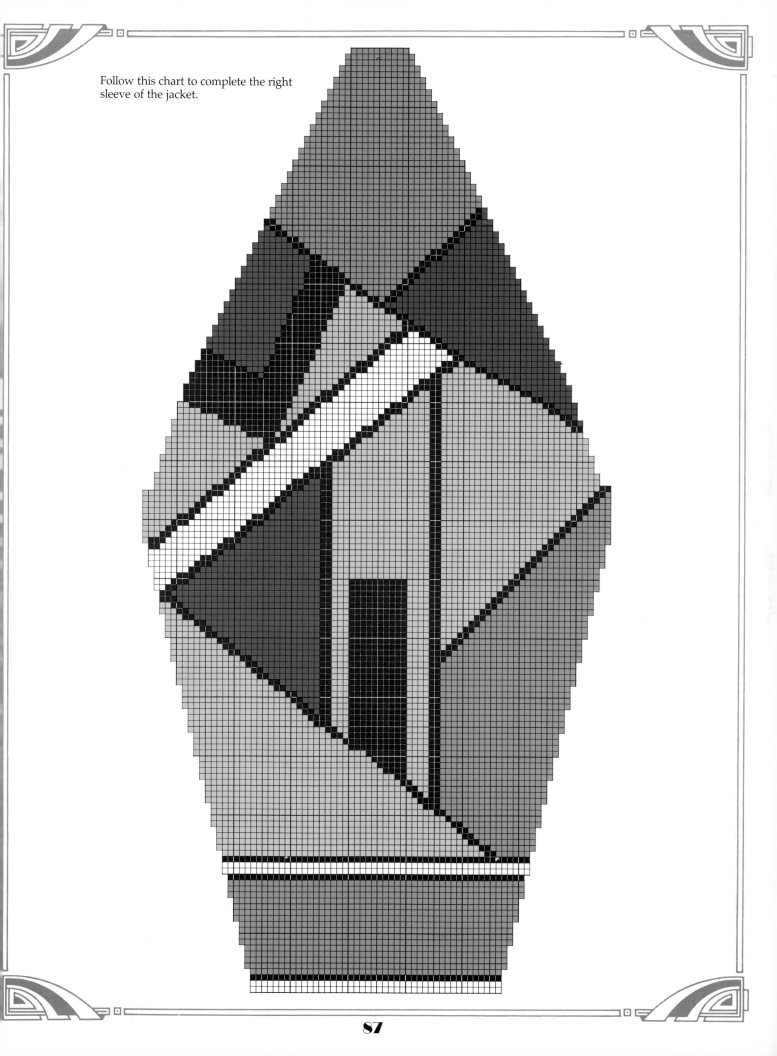

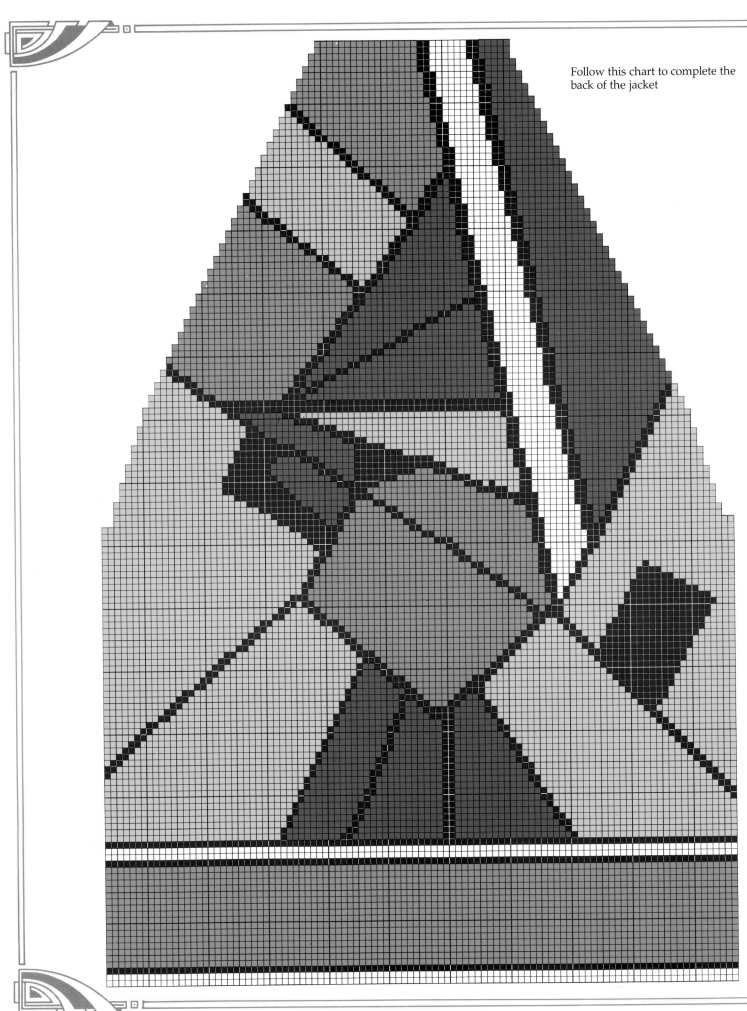

Follow this chart to complete the
back of the jacket

Follow this chart to complete the left
and right fronts of the jacket.

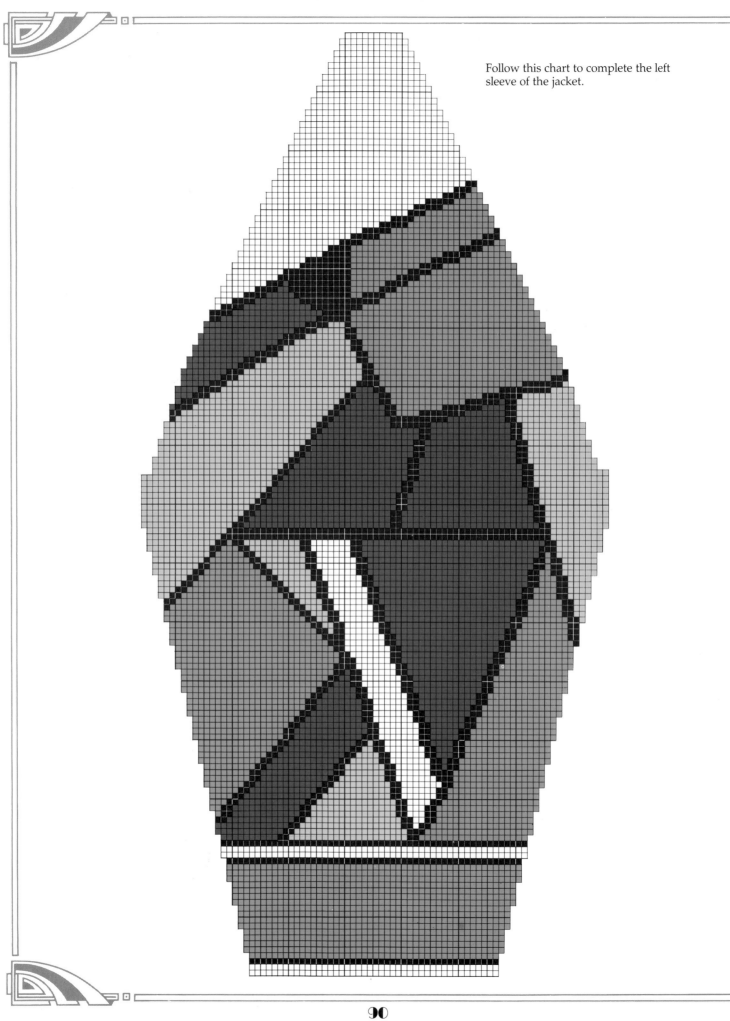

Follow this chart to complete the left sleeve of the jacket.

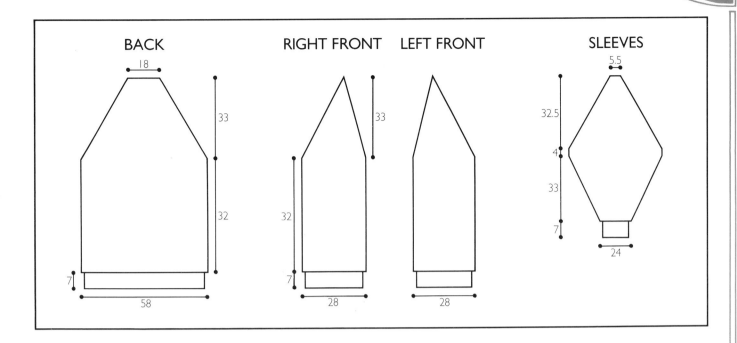

BACK	RIGHT FRONT	LEFT FRONT	SLEEVES

BACK: 18, 33, 32, 7, 58

RIGHT FRONT: 33, 32, 7, 28

LEFT FRONT: 28

SLEEVES: 5.5, 32.5, 4, 33, 7, 24

chart, inc 1 st at each end of the 5th row and every following 4th row until you have 82 sts. Work 9 rows from chart without shaping. **Shape raglans:** keeping chart correct, cast off 2 sts at beg of next 2 rows, work 1 row, then dec 1 st at each end of next and every 3rd row 5 times, then dec 1 st at each end of every alt row until 10 sts remain. Cast off all sts.

LEFT SLEEVE

Work rib as for right sleeve. Change to 5mm needles and work from left sleeve chart, working sleeve increases and raglan decreases as for right sleeve.

SHAWL COLLAR (right side)

Using a flat seam, join all raglan seams. With RS facing, 4mm needles and blue, pick up and k 77 sts up right front edge to beg of front shaping, 72 sts up front shaping, 10 sts from sleeve top and 16 sts to finish at centre back neck. Work in k2, p2 rib for 3 rows.

Buttonhole row (bottom edge at start of next row): rib 3 (cast off 2 sts, rib 12) 6 times, rib to end.

Next row: work in rib, casting on 2 sts over each group of 2 cast-off sts. Work 2 more rows in rib.

Next row: cast off 76 sts in rib for buttonhole band, work in k2, p2 rib on remaining sts. Work 1 row in rib, then cast off 4 sts at beg of next row. Rep these last 2 rows until 15 sts remain. Work 1 row, cast off remaining sts.

SHAWL COLLAR (left side)

Work as for right side, reversing all shapings and omitting buttonholes.

MAKING UP

Join side and sleeve seams using a narrow back-stitch. Sew buttons to match buttonholes.

Rhodanthe

Introduced in 1934 "Rhodanthe" used a new style of decoration. Rather than have bold colours clearly separated by an outline, similar shades were 'etched' onto the ware by overlapping brushstrokes and colours. "Rhodanthe" was the orange colourway of this design, there was also a pink version, "Viscaria", and eventually a green/blue one, "Aurea". "Rhodanthe" was produced on numerous pieces of tableware and teaware sets; here it is shown on a "Lotus" jug.

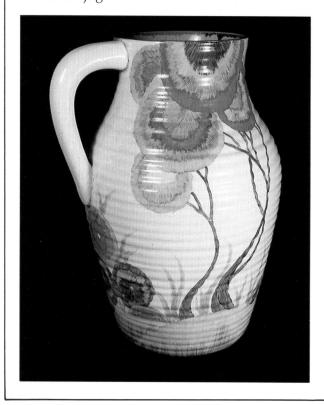

"Rhodanthe" is featured here on a luxurious batwing angora and silk cardigan, which is worked using the intarsia method.

LEFT FRONT

Using 2¾mm needles and black silk, cast on 60 sts. K1, p1 rib for 4 rows. Change to orange, rib 4 rows. Change to gold, rib 4 rows. Change to black and cont in rib until work measures 9cm, ending with a RS row. Inc 28 sts evenly across the next row of rib (88 sts)*.

Change to 3¼mm needles and black angora and commence following chart in st st working 30 rows without shaping. Next row (RS): inc 1 st at beg of this row and the 6 following 3rd rows, then inc 1 st at same edge on the next 30 alt rows. *At the same time*, when you have 117 sts on your needle, **shape neck:** next row (WS): dec 1 st at beg of this row and the 26 following 3rd rows. When your side edge shaping is complete and you have 120 sts on your needle, **shape sleeves:** next row (RS): cast on 12 sts at beg of this row and the following 2 alt rows, then cast on 13 sts on the following alt row. Work straight at armhole edge, cont neck decreases until they are complete. Work 8 rows without shaping, leave sts on a spare needle.

POCKET LINING

Using 3¼mm needles and black silk, cast on 45 sts. Work in st st for 40 rows, leave sts on a spare needle.

RIGHT FRONT

Work rib as for left front to *. Change to 3¼mm needles and black angora and work as for left front in black only, reversing all shapings. *At the same time*, when you have completed your 5th increase and there are 93 sts on your needle, **make pocket opening:** next row (RS): k18, leave the next 45 sts on a stitch holder, k to end. On the return row, p30, p across 45 sts held for pocket lining, p to end. When right front is complete, leave sts on a spare needle.

BACK

Using 2¾mm needles and black silk, cast on 128 sts. Work in rib as for front, inc 58 sts evenly across last

MATERIALS
Melinda Coss angora – black: 280gm; Melinda Coss tussah silk – orange: 25gm; grey: 25gm; gold: 20gm; ecru: 20gm; black: 20gm.
6 buttons 1½cm in diameter.

NEEDLES
One pair of 2¾mm and one pair of 3¼mm needles.
One stitch holder.

TENSION
Using 3¼mm needles and measured over st st, 28 sts and 36 rows = 10cm square.

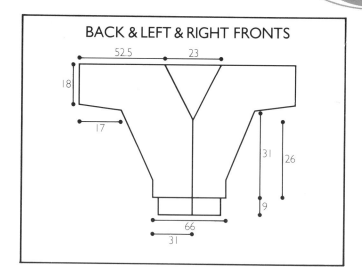

BACK & LEFT & RIGHT FRONTS

Follow this chart to complete the left front of the cardigan.

row of rib. Change to 3¼mm needles and black angora and work 30 rows in st st. Inc 1 st at each end of the next row and the 6 following third rows, then inc 1 st at each end on the next 30 alt rows. **Shape sleeves:** cast on 12 sts at beg of next 6 rows, then cast on 13 sts at beg of next 2 rows. Work straight until back matches fronts in length ending with a RS row. Turn to wrong side and lay back over corresponding fronts with RSs facing. Starting at the cuff edge, knit tog and cast off corresponding front. Cast off centre 64 sts, knit tog and cast off remaining 147 sts of back and second front.

POCKET TOP
Using 2¾mm needles and orange, pick up the 45 sts held for pocket top and work 2 rows in k1, p1 rib. Change to gold, rib 2 rows. Cast off in gold. Neatly stitch pocket lining and welt into position.

BUTTONBAND
Using 2¾mm needles and black silk, cast on 13 sts.
Row 1: sl 1, (k1, p1) 5 times, k2.
Row 2: sl 1, (p1, k1) 5 times, p2.
Cont working in rib as set until buttonband fits neatly, when slightly stretched, from the bottom of the left front, across the back neck and down to the bottom of the right front neck shaping. Stitch

partially finished band into position and mark 6 buttonhole positions with pins, placing the first pin 2½cm from bottom of band and last pin just before the neck shaping with remaining 4 pins spaced evenly between. Cont working buttonband in rib, making buttonholes to correspond with pins as follows: sl 1, k1, p1, k1, pl, cast off 3 sts in rib, rib to end. On return row cast on 3 sts over those previously cast off. Cont in rib until band fits neatly to bottom rib edge. Cast off.

CUFFS
Using 2¾mm needles and black silk, pick up every other stitch (65 sts) along cuff edge. Next row: k1, p2 tog,* k1, p1, k1, p2 tog. Rep to last 2 sts, k2 (52 sts). Rib 4 rows, change to gold, dec 1 st at each end of the next row and every following 8th row until you have 44 sts. *At the same time*, when you have completed 4 rows of rib in gold, change to orange and rib 4 rows, then change to black and cont until decrease rows are complete. Rib 7 rows. Cast off using a 3¼mm needle.

MAKING UP
Join ribs, sides and sleeves with a flat seam. Sew buttonhole band neatly into position. Sew on buttons.

ABBREVIATIONS

alt	alternate(ly)
beg	begin(ning)
C2L	k 2nd st behind first st, then k first st, slipping both sts off needle together.
C6F	cable 6 forward – i.e., slip first 3 sts onto a cable needle and hold at front of work, k 2nd 3 sts, k 3 sts from cable needle.
C6B	cable 6 back – i.e., slip first 3 sts onto a cable needle and hold at back of work, k 2nd 3 sts, k 3 sts from cable needle.
cm	centimetre(s)
cont	continue/continuing
dec	decrease/decreasing
inc	increase/increasing
k	knit
M1	make 1 – i.e., pick up loop between 2 sts and knit.
moss st	k1, p1 to end of row. On return row, p the k st and k the p st.
p	purl
rep	repeat
RS	right side
sl	slip
st(s)	stitch(es)
st st	stocking stitch
tog	together
WS	wrong side

ACKNOWLEDGEMENTS

Clothes and Accessories

Antiquarius – dress, page 86
Beaux Bijou – beads, page 34; brooch, page 23; earrings, page 93; necklace, pages 23, 56, 93
Eavis & Brown – dress, page 23
Fina – scarf, page 34
Pamela Haywood – dress, pages 67, 93
The Hat Shop – hats, pages 15, 29, 63, 67, 71, 77, 83
Cornelia James – gloves, page 45
Next – culottes, page 45; dress, page 77; jodhpurs, page 51; maroon skirt, page 83; scarf, page 45; shirt, pages 19, 56; trousers, pages 29, 56
Persiflage – sequin skullcap, page 23
Ellen Pollock – beads, page 83
The Purple Shop – beads, page 39; bracelets, page 10
Risky Business – bag, page 19; basket, page 34; binoculars, page 71; camera, page 45; flask, page 86; gloves, page 59; golf bag, page 29; hamper, page 86; hat, pages 19, 34; parasol, page 77; riding crop, page 51; riding hat, page 51; shooting stick page 63; telescope, page 15; umbrella, pages 39, 83
Jeri Scott – earrings, page 10

Make-up and Hair Jo Gillingwater at Artistic Licence
Models – Varian and Nadja at Premier and Matthew Gardiner at Models 1
Photography Liz McAulay assisted by Alex
Styling Bo Chapman at Artistic Licence

YARN INFORMATION

All the sample garments illustrated in this book were knitted in Melinda Coss yarns. As many of the designs contain small quantities of several different colours, Melinda Coss offers individual kits containing only the quantities of yarn necessary to complete each garment. Each kit contains enough yarn to knit up to the largest size indicated on the pattern; in addition, zips, buttons, embroidery threads and trimmings are included where appropriate.

To order, contact Melinda Coss at No. 1 Copenhagen Street, London N1 0JB or telephone her on 01-833-3929.

For those who wish to substitute different yarns, weights are given throughout to the nearest 50gm ball. To obtain the best results you must ensure that the tension recommended on your selected yarn *matches the tension* printed in our pattern. We cannot guarantee your results if this rule is not followed.

PICTURE CREDITS

From the collection of Julie Bass and David Metcalfe page 55; from the collection of Jill and Jack Gertson page 85; from the collections of Jill and Jack Gertson, and Leonard R. Griffin page 76; from the collection of Leonard R. Griffin pages 9, 38, 58, 62; from the collection of Muir Hewitt pages 70, 83; from the collections of Muir Hewitt and Leonard R. Griffin page 44; from the collection of Pauline and David Latham page 28; from a private collection page 50; from a private collection page 92.